Testimo

Sinnott reminds us that we are only stewards of the enterprise and that our satisfaction will come not from tailoring it to our needs but from addressing the needs of those we serve. Well done, Dan. This is a must-read for Boards and leadership teams alike. Succession planning is not an option; it is a mandate!

Thomas E. Beeman, PhD, FACHE
President and Chief Executive Officer
Lancaster General Health
Rear Admiral, SHCE, USN

Sinnott possesses a rare combination of high business acumen and outstanding communication skills. He blends these proficiencies effortlessly in his latest business allegory on the important subject of succession planning. This book should be on every executives' "must read" list.

John C. Wagner
President
Construction Risk Solutions, LLC.

Sinnott reminds us that a core competency of leadership is to plan for the organization's sustainability and enduring success. This powerful story effectively demonstrates the critical nature of a thoughtful succession process. It's a vital read for senior management and governing boards.

David Shulkin MD
President,
Morristown Medical Center

The hardest part in reading Sinnott's second fable is to be patient enough to finish a chapter before rushing to put the ideas into practice. The Intersection keeps the message simple and focused, and shines a bright light on the fundamental importance of getting the succession plan right.

Daniel Costello
President and Chief Executive Officer
AIA Life Korea

THE
INTERSECTION

ENSURING THE FUTURE OF YOUR BUSINESS AND
CAREER THROUGH SUCCESSION PLANNING

DANIEL J. SINNOTT

ISBN: 978-0-9911477-0-0

For information, contact Daniel J. Sinnott, Sinnott Executive Consulting, 319 Hampton Road, Wilmington, DE 19803, (302) 656-2898

This book is dedicated to my "bride" Gail and my three loving children Dan Jr, Devin, Jacqueline and my two sisters, Peggy and Mary.

Acknowledgements

———•———

I would like to thank my editor Suzanne Murray from StyleMatters Writing Services for her patience and diligence throughout this entire process. I would also like to thank Chloe Westman for proofreading the final document and also for her feedback and support. Finally I would like to thank the following individuals who so graciously gave of their time and provided their perspective while conducting research on this book:

Thomas E. Beeman, PhD, FACHE
President and Chief Executive Officer
Lancaster General Health
Rear Admiral, SHCE, USN

R. Michael Buckley, MD
Executive Director
Pennsylvania Hospital
University of Pennsylvania Health System

Timothy J. Constantine
President
Highmark Blue Cross Blue Shield Delaware

Susan Croushore
Former President & Chief Executive Officer
Christ Hospital

Jeffery Drop
Senior Vice President
Catholic Health Initiatives

Michael J. Duncan
President & Chief Executive Officer
The Chester County Hospital and Health System
University of Pennsylvania Health System

Will Ferniany, Ph.D.
Chief Executive Officer
University of Alabama at Birmingham

J. Gary Langmuir
President & Chief Executive Officer
Wohlsen Construction Company

Patricia Maryland, Dr.PH
President of Healthcare Operations and Chief Operating Officer
Ascension Health

John Morahan
President & Chief Executive Officer
St. Joseph Regional Health Network

Judy Persichilli,
President & Chief Executive Officer
Catholic Health East

Michael A. Rashid
President & Chief Executive Officer
AmeriHealth Caritas

Nancy M. Schlichting
Chief Executive Officer
Henry Ford Health System

David J. Shulkin, MD
President
Morristown Medical Center

Michael A. Slubowski
President & Chief Executive Officer
Sisters of Charity of Leavenworth Health System

Paul A. Spaude
President & Chief Executive Officer
Borgess Health

Richard J. Statuto
President & Chief Executive Officer
Bon Secours Health System

Ronald W. Swinford, MD
President & Chief Executive Officer
Lehigh Valley Health Network

Christine W. Winn
Executive Director
Aria Health - Torresdale Campus

TABLE OF CONTENTS

1

Sometimes Bad Things Happen to Good People

S EAN O'BRIEN LIKED routines that made certain parts of his life simple. For example, his drive into work had been the same over the past sixteen years. He would always take the same route, which included going through mostly quiet neighborhoods with red brick row homes just to avoid the early morning traffic on the major highways to Divine Mercy Hospital, where he was CEO. Along the way, he would pass the grade school crossing guard, to whom he would always say or wave hello. He also enjoyed stopping at Joe's Diner for a 10 oz. cup of real coffee, to go, and not some of that boutique swill that cost so much. But for some reason, on this late May day, Sean was seeing the ride into work very differently than any other time over the past sixteen years.

As Sean turned the corner to enter the hospital parking garage, he saw something that really set him off: a large, multi-colored canvas banner strung between two lampposts and flapping in the wind. Sean, approaching Luther

Jackson, Manager of Security for the hospital, rolled down his window and barked to his friend, "Take that goddamn sign down." The sign read,

Happy Retirement, Sean O'Brien! Thank you for your years of service!

Luther was standing at his normal spot, where each morning outside of the employee garage he made sure that every hospital employee, patient, and visitor got in safe and sound. A retired Chicago police officer, Luther knew a great deal about the community and how to keep Divine Mercy a safe place. As Sean waved his monthly parking card across the electronic reader, Luther said, "Now Sean, you know if I take that sign down, you are going to upset all of the doctors and employees who are really going to miss you after today."

"Fine, keep it up, Luther," Sean reluctantly agreed. "But only until the end of the day." It would be Sean's last as CEO of Divine Mercy Hospital.

Once inside the cool confines of the hospital, Sean spent his day putting his things in boxes and returning calls from people in the community who wanted to thank him for all he had done for the community. Of the many employees who stopped by to wish him well, Mike Polaski, a COO from another hospital within the Health System, offered to help carry some of the boxes out to his car. Sean politely declined, though he would probably regret that decision later in the day.

In addition to the family photos he was packing up, Sean treasured most the files containing letters from patients and the hospital employees that he had received over the years, sharing stories about how the hospital had helped them in a time of need. These letters were for Sean a subtle but powerful recognition of the great work he and his organization had done for the community. Sean always said he would spend his time in retirement rereading the letters, and now that time had come.

The highlight of the day for Sean was the "Going Away Tea" that had become a tradition when someone of importance was leaving the organization. This tradition dated back well over 100 years, with the founding religious order of nuns who wanted to thank those who had helped make their hospital a success. As part of the tradition, the medical staff, employees, and community members were invited to enjoy good food, nonalcoholic drinks, and the friendly company of one another.

Sean arrived right on time at 3PM and was shocked as he entered the Murray Conference Center at how many people were present: The center was designed to hold five hundred people comfortably, and the room appeared to be near capacity. He always felt he had made a difference at the hospital; seeing so many in attendance at the tea made him realize that it was true. Still, amidst the goodwill he was feeling at the sight of all these caring people, Sean could not help but feel a pang of anger as he noticed what he had coined the "Liars Club" off in a corner, a group of leaders from the Health System that he had come to know all too well for their lack of integrity and egotistical attitudes. The Liars Club membership included Miles Greene, the Holy Spirit Health System CEO; Tina Blake, the Health System CFO; Steve Driver, the Health System Chief Human Resource Officer; and finally Charles Brown, a Holy Spirit Health System Board member as well as a Divine Mercy Board member. Sean wondered how many of those in the group couldn't wait to have the tea end versus those who would enjoy watching him take leave of the hospital on this his final day.

As for Charles Brown, he looked like he could still play defensive end for his 1984 high school state championship football team. While he was blessed with a congenial personality, Brown (at six feet, four inches and 245 pounds) was not afraid to use physical force to get his way. In fact, a legend from Brown's high school years still followed him to this day. It was during the final semester of his senior year when Brown chose not to study for his final math exam. Even so, he had the confidence he would do well on the exam anyway because he had "assurances" from a student named Alan Krigstein that Brown could cheat off of Alan during the exam. In return, Krigstein would not suffer any bodily harm.

But then something happened. The day of the exam, Krigstein changed his mind and backed out of the deal. As a result, Brown failed the final. Even with failing, he was allowed to graduate because of the extra credit he did for his math teacher, who just happened to be his football coach. For his decision, though, Krigstein ended up in the Emergency Room with a broken nose and eleven stitches to close a cut on his head. The only thing positive that came out of that decision for Krigstein was a saying his father shared later that night, "Someday, bad people like Brown will get what is coming to them."

After the attack, Brown's reputation as a "bad ass" seemed to grow larger by the day, and he took full advantage of this newfound popularity, including eventually becoming a Councilman of the City of Chicago, which was what later landed him on the Divine Mercy Hospital and Holy Spirit Health System Boards. His role on the Board was due to a questionable set of circumstances that only Sean knew. As Sean often said to his Executive Assistant Erin Carey, "I hate slimy politicians."

Brown may have had bad things coming to him, as Alan Krigstein's father had once said, but today didn't appear to be that day. It was Sean who was being ousted from the hospital system. Although Brown's involvement in the Board as of late had been minimal due to frequent out-of-state travel, Brown still had plenty of power to pull strings when he needed to, and Sean was sure he had played some role in Sean's termination.

Sean had coined the name for the Liar's Club several years ago when he noticed at Health System meetings and functions that these individuals all seemed to advocate for decisions that were self-serving, rather than for the best of the Health System and the community. They would regularly bend morals, blur integrity, and speak convenient manipulations of fact in order to get their way. And, of course, they always stuck together, finding a way to support each other's self-serving initiatives.

After Miles Greene backed out of a verbal commitment to fund a community health van to serve the poor neighborhoods surrounding the hospital, an initiative that Sean later learned Charles Brown opposed, Sean realized that Greene and the others could never be trusted. The Liars Club seemed to all work together to make Sean's life and that of many of the other executives within the Health System hospitals "hell." At the same time, Sean made it his "cause celeb" to push back on these four fools as much and as often as he could. And he did so successfully, like the time that he refused to use some of his hospital financial reserves to help the Health System reach its bottom line financial goal for the year just so that Greene, Blake, and Driver would get their annual incentive compensation checks.

Unfortunately, although Sean had won many battles with the Liars Club, it seemed that perhaps they had won the war. Sean was certain that Blake, Driver, and Brown all had a hand in forcing him out, although this was a secret known to only a few in the organization. Other than the Liars Club, no one else in the room knew that Sean's retirement was forced. If he had had his choice, he would have stayed as the CEO of Divine Mercy Hospital for several more years.

As Sean walked toward the punch bowl, Miles Greene, the "leader" of the Liars Club, approached. Sean's shoulders tightened.

"Helloooo," Miles said to Sean, extending his hand as if to shake. But when Sean reached out in return to maintain a façade of politeness, Miles pulled his hand away. "Gotcha!" Miles said with a grin.

Miles added, "I hope you have something fun scheduled for the first several months of your 'retirement,'" to which Sean added, "Nothing yet, but I'm sure I will come up with something good."

Sean then added, "You know what, Miles? Let's not pretend we like one another anymore. We both know that if it wasn't for the Sisters' tradition of throwing one of these Teas, you'd not be here to say goodbye to me. You'd be in your office planning a dinner with Blake, Driver, and Brown to celebrate my departure."

"I don't know what it is your talking about," Miles said with a mock straight face.

Sean replied, "We all know how you like to play nice in front of the good Sisters and then how when they are not around your true colors come out." Good old Sean, still telling it like it was, even on his last day on the job.

Finally, Maryanne Richmond came over to break up the tension between Sean and Miles. Having worked side by side with Sean for many years, she knew of the true dislike Sean had for Miles. Maryanne was the Divine Mercy COO who was replacing Sean as CEO of the hospital, effective at the end of today. Maryanne had grown to love Sean as a person and hold him in high esteem as a leader as she watched him over the years improve the hospital's reputation within the community, upgrade the quality of care provided, and successfully turn around a struggling organization.

Maryanne gave Sean a big hug and said warmly, "Congratulations on this next phase! We are all going to miss you so much."

Miles grumbled to himself and walked toward the dessert table, where the rest of the Liars Club was now hovering. "So, are you ready to hit the ground running on Monday?" Sean asked Maryanne.

"I don't know…do you think I'm ready?" Maryanne asked, returning Sean's question with a question.

Sean smiled reassuringly. "Maryanne," he said, "You have all the talent you need to be successful—as long as you are willing to take some risks and learn from your mistakes. The one thing I have learned in life is that the more you risk, the more you will gain."

Maryanne tilted her head to one side as she pondered Sean's response.

"And I'm just one phone call away if you need any help," Sean said. He knew that Maryanne had many of the tools she needed to become a strong leader, especially her authentic and diplomatic way of interacting with other people. And, yet, he also knew of Maryanne's tendency to let others overstep their boundaries at times because she was such a nice person. She hated to say no if she didn't have to, and she truly saw the best in everyone, giving them the benefit of the doubt whenever she could.

Maryanne was born and raised in Tawas City, Michigan, located in the Lower Peninsula along Lake Huron. Her father, Mike, had worked his entire career in a foundry that made springs for the Ford Motor Company until he retired, while her mother, Sharon, had been a fourth-grade public school teacher up until last year. Maryanne was one of five children who took advantage of her strong skills in math and science to become a nurse. Sean loved that Maryanne came from a strong family environment that valued hard work and honesty. She had the integrity, work ethic, and strong people skills to make an excellent CEO, and he was thrilled to have her be his replacement, given the circumstances.

Still, in the back of Sean's mind, he wished he had some more time to help develop Maryanne for the challenges that lay ahead. If he had had more control over the situation, he would have given her a few more years as COO before mentoring her to look for a CEO position. What's more, with the Liars Club running around the hospital system, Maryanne would have plenty of landmines waiting ahead. Sean wondered if Maryanne would have enough responsible colleagues and staff members to help her effectively execute her vision for Divine Mercy. He knew that promoting someone into a new role without the proper support increased their chances of failing.

He had also learned many years ago that "the skills that get you into the job will not be the skills that keep you in the job." So even though Maryanne had been successful in the past as COO, she would likely need to develop a whole new set of competencies to excel as CEO.

Even with this concern, Sean knew that he did not have any choice but to leave Divine Mercy and that it was Maryanne's time to take her "shot" at being a hospital CEO.

Just then, as Sean saw Tina Blake in an apparent heated conversation with one of her direct reports, he had a flashback to a meeting he had had several years ago that made him realize things had dramatically changed in his Health System. At the time, he was in a budget review meeting with his CFO and several individuals from the corporate finance staff, including Tina Blake (System CFO) and Maria Smith (System Controller). The Health System for the past several years had been pushing Sean and his team to produce more of a bottom line to carry the losses posted by the other hospitals in the Health System.

During this particular meeting, Maria Smith threatened, "If you do not produce a bigger profit next year, we will put you on 'hospice capital,'" meaning that Divine Mercy Hospital would have no new money to invest in new services or equipment. This comment sent Sean's CFO into a rage, resulting in a yelling match between Maria and the CFO. Sean watched with interest as Tina Blake, Maria's boss, just let the heated argument play out while it looked like Blake was enjoying the fight. Finally, Sean intervened, stating that this item would be decided not by the people in the room but in discussions between his Board Chair, and Miles Greene, the Health System CEO.

Sean knew the "hospice capital" plan would limit his hospital's ability to produce a bigger bottom line, which the Health System desperately needed. He wondered if it was a bluff. Hard to say. He also knew such a plan would severely hurt his reputation with members of his executive team and medical staff who were expecting the money to purchase new equipment and develop new services. He wouldn't put it past the Liars Club to purposely be setting him up for failure.

After the meeting, Sean's CFO vented in private to Sean. "If Maria was a guy," he said, "I would kick her ass from here to Canarse."

"My big concern," Sean said, "is that we will see more of this behavior from the system leadership as they get more pressure to produce a stronger bottom line." After that meeting, Sean began to lose some of his passion for being a hospital CEO.

Several months after the incident, Miles Greene called Sean for a special meeting and asked for Sean's resignation. "You've worn out your welcome with the corporate staff and some of the Board members," Miles told him.

Sean laughed to himself since he knew it was the Liars Club that finally had enough leverage and support to force Sean out. Sean also knew it was Brown who was massaging certain members of the Board to support this effort. Brown's stature with Greene and some of the board members had grown recently since Brown was instrumental in getting $22 million in additional annual funding for the Holy Spirit Health System from the State of Illinois to help offset losses from treating so many Medicaid patients with no insurance. As time went on, Sean became more of an irritant to the Liars Club and some of the Board due to his straight-shooting talk and pull-no-punches attitude, and it was positioned that to secure the future of Divine Mercy Hospital, it was time for a change in the CEO role.

As for today's Tea, it was at Sean's insistence that there be no more than three people speaking at his going away, including Sean himself. Sean also told his executive assistant, Erin Carey, who was responsible for planning the event, that he did not want anyone from the Corporate Office to speak since he knew they would say the "right" things in public to burnish their reputations but not actually mean a word of it. He did not want to give them that pleasure.

First to speak was Maryanne. Maryanne knew Sean did not have the type of personality that had to be fussed about at public gatherings so she kept her comments brief. Then she called Sean up to the podium and quietly handed him an envelope and went on to explain that the Medical Staff, the hospital Executive and Management Teams, and many of the employees had chipped in for an all-expenses-paid, four-week golf vacation to Ireland for Sean. "We even took the liberty of booking your flights and making your hotel reservations beginning four weeks from today," Maryanne said, "since we know after today your calendar is wide open." That comment got quite a laugh from the audience.

Sean was stunned by the gift but, more importantly, by the generosity of so many people. He always felt he was making a difference at the hospital and in the lives of those he worked with, but this gift of their appreciation still caught him off guard. "Thank you," Sean said as he looked at the sea of smiling faces around him. He wondered if they could see that his eyes were a bit watery.

Maryanne replied, "We all just felt you needed to take a long break given all of your years of service. Sean, please know how much you meant to this place and to so many people whose lives you have touched over your sixteen years at Divine Mercy. This hospital and many of us, including me, would not be where we are if it was not for you." After Maryanne finished her comments, she and Sean hugged while all those in attendance applauded.

Maryanne added quietly to Sean, "One of the reasons why people were so generous is because you haven't taken any time off since Kate died." The last reference to his wife made Sean realize that since Kate's death three years ago, he had just thrown himself into his work as a way of coping with his loss.

Sean replied, "I guess you are right. I have been going at it pretty hard for several years now, and I probably need to get off this treadmill and decompress for a while." What Maryanne and everyone else did not know was just how much Sean still missed his bride Kate.

As Sean was waving to those in the audience, Maryanne gave Sean one last big hug, and just then the tears began to flow down her face. Seeing the tears, Sean whispered to Maryanne, "You are going to do great things for this hospital. Remember to keep working on the tools we've always talked about." Sean was referring to the Career Triangle and the Leadership Equation, two models he used while mentoring Maryanne over the past several years as a way to not only develop her business and leadership skills but to also make sure she had some type of balance in her life.

The next person to speak was Sean's favorite community member, Lilly Black. Lilly was a prominent member of the African American community and had been a member of the Divine Mercy Hospital Board for fourteen of the sixteen years that Sean had been CEO.

Lilly began by saying, "When my adopted son, Sean O'Brien, first arrived at Divine Mercy, the hospital was in a heap of trouble. We were on the verge of closing and the quality of the care we were providing to our community was terrible. Many of us thought, 'How is this skinny Irish kid from the Roscoe Village section of Chicago going to save us? But with a great deal of hard work and determination, he began to turn this place around. Hard decisions had to be made like closing our OB unit. Many inside and outside the hospital were against this decision but that all changed when Sean told a packed auditorium, 'There is nothing worse than being really good at doing the wrong thing.'"

"Sure, our OB service had okay quality outcomes," Lilly continued, "but we were losing millions of dollars a year. It was a tough decision that Sean made, but the right decision."

Although some in the room had not agreed with Sean's decision, many respected his conviction and his courage. The decision to close the OB unit was made somewhat easier since all of the Obstetric and Pediatric physicians would still have their offices at the hospital and arrangements were made with the hospital less than a half mile away to handle all of the deliveries from Divine Mercy. People learned by observing Sean over time that he always balanced the community's health needs with the financial needs of the hospital.

Lilly continued, "Many leaders would not have had the guts and courage to make that decision, let alone be out in public explaining and defending it. Yet, Sean did. It was soon after that that the hospital began its successful turnaround and grew to be one of the top hospitals in the State of Illinois."

The room broke into a round of applause. Sean and Lilly hugged, and Lilly whispered, "You know that Kate is smiling in Heaven on this blessed day, happy to see that you are finally going to get some time to relax with the knowledge that 'you done good.' God Bless you, son."

Sean then took to the podium and began by responding to some of Lilly's comments. "Thank you for your kind words, Lilly. Do you remember at my first board meeting how everyone ganged up on me, demanding to know how I was going to save their hospital? It was at that point that I started to question my decision to accept this job. But then, Lilly, you stood up and said, 'Divine Mercy did not get into this sorry state overnight and it will not get out of it overnight. We must give this young man a chance to figure things out.' From that night on, Lilly and I formed a special bond, which I will never forget."

Sean turned his attention to everyone in the audience. "As many of you know, I am not a man of many words, especially when it comes to talking about myself. I was raised to let your actions speak for themselves, and I hope we can all rejoice in the many great things we have accomplished together over the past sixteen years. Early in my tenure here, I learned that things don't get done just because the CEO says so. Someone needs to carry out the decision, and I have been truly blessed to work with so many talented and wonderful individuals. The only thing I ask of you is to keep up the burning desire to continue to make Divine Mercy a beacon of hope for this community. I will cherish our time together and I will keep you in my daily prayers. Thank you for all of your dedication and support, and God bless."

Most in the group were already standing, but those who had taken a chair now stood up. Everyone was clapping: the old-timers feeling proud of the skinny Irish kid who had grown up, the younger folks like Maryanne grateful for all of Sean's mentorship, and the community members who had had faith in both Sean and Lilly Black that everything would work out just fine. Sean touched his hand to his heart and then extended it toward the group as a gesture of gratitude.

The Tea had come to an end, so Sean quickly walked to the main exit door so he could say goodbye to as many people as possible. He was not surprised that the first group he met there was all four members of the Liars Club. "Leaving so soon?" Sean asked. They all mumbled in different ways about how they had to get back to work, although Sean highly doubted that any of them would be putting forth too much effort given their track records, especially Charles Brown. He was the kind of person who did everything he could to avoid working hard.

Before Sean stepped out of their way, he asked, "What do you and the 1919 Chicago Black Sox's have in common?" Sean was referring to the team that participated in the most famous baseball scandal in the history of the game. There was no answer from the stunned individuals, and then Sean added, "Just like the eight members of the Chicago Black Sox's who cheated, you four clowns will not even know when your careers are over until it is too late." Sean thought, "What the hell, one last shot at this motley group."

It was Brown who spoke up and said, "That will never happen to any of us because we all take care of one another."

2

THE WALK ABOUT

I T WAS A month since Sean had left Divine Mercy Hospital, and now he
was at O'Hare International airport, sitting at the gate for Flight #1772,
waiting to begin his four-week golf vacation to Ireland. Sean walked
throughout the airport, mostly people-watching, a practice he liked to do
before any long flight. It helped him to keep both his mind and his body
engaged while also helping with his fear of flying.

As Sean looked down at his small carry-on, he chuckled as he remembered how Maryanne Richmond had reminded him to make sure he didn't
have any liquids that were more than six ounces in his bag. She had stopped
by last night to see how his packing was coming along, knowing that in the
past it was Kate who had made sure everything was arranged and organized.
Sean was grateful for Maryanne's support as well as that of so many others
from the hospital.

Sean still could not believe the generosity of the Divine Mercy "family"
for raising the money to pay for this extravagant trip. All expenses were covered, including a limo to and from the airport. They even included 500 euros

to help with some of his spending money. Sean had never been on a trip this long, and it reminded him of some of his Australians buddies who every so many years would go on a six-week holiday or "walkabout."

Sean pulled a wrapped gift out of his carry-on, but before he could open it, something on the overhead television caught his eye. It only took a second for him to focus in and discover a photo of Miles Greene, with the head-line, *Local Exec Fired!* stamped across the Holy Spirit Health System CEO's face. Sean jumped up from his seat and stepped closer to the screen so he could hear what the newscaster was saying. The report stated that Greene was charged with overseeing the submission of fraudulent hospital quality outcome data to the Federal Government for several years, resulting in major losses and possible Federal fines and penalties and indicated that he had been relieved of his duties as CEO immediately.

"So the house of cards begins to tumble," Sean thought. He wondered if any of the other members of the Liars Club would get caught up in this investigation. He suspected that Brown had had a role in things. Sean often thought it was Brown who was putting significant pressure on Greene to make the Health System look better than it was, to increase Brown's own political power. Regardless of Brown's likely involvement, Sean figured that Brown was already using his political influence to keep his name out of the investigation. It would be interesting to see where this all led.

A voice came over the airport loud speaker; it was time to board. Sean broke his gaze from the television and returned to his carry-on, so he could put the unwrapped gift away and get ready to board. "How will it all turn out?" he thought. With that question, Sean made a decision not to think about the Health System for a long while but to concentrate instead on relaxing and enjoying this gift of a trip to Ireland. Within minutes, he was on the plane, buckling up, and ordering his favorite drink—a virgin Bloody Mary—from a beautiful Irish flight attendant, named Molly Kennedy.

About an hour into the flight while some around him slept and others watched movies, Sean pulled out the wrapped gift from Erin Carey. At Sean's farewell Tea, she had given it to him with a card that read, "To be opened on your flight to Ireland. Remember the line found on the very first page." Sean pulled the wrapping paper away from the taped seam and turned the book over to reveal its title, *Travels with Charlie* by John Steinbeck. It was just like Erin to find him the perfect gift. Sean opened the hardback to the first page and read the very lines that Erin had wanted him to see: "You do not take a trip, a trip takes you," the sentence read.

As Sean found this special line, it made him begin to wonder what might happen while he was in Ireland. He liked the idea of getting away, and yet he didn't know what it would be like to have so much time on his hands. He started to think about several of the places he hoped to visit while in the country—The Cliff of Moher, The Glencar Falls in Sligo, and a hike to the top of Slieve League in the County of Donegal—and then he felt a pang of sadness and guilt as he thought about the fact that his wife, Kate, should have been on this trip with him.

The two met while Sean was in graduate school working on his MBA in Health Administration. Kate was a physical therapist and found Sean to be charming and very rugged and handsome. They married two years later and spent their honeymoon in Ireland. Kate said it was a "trip of a lifetime," with Sean promising that someday they would return.

Over the years, Sean often spoke about taking Kate back to Ireland, but it always seemed like life got in the way. Two children, work, and then Kate's health problems made their thirty-six years married seem to go by like "smoke through a keyhole." Sean also found it hard to believe he was sixty-two years old; he certainly did not feel that age.

It was a year before Kate's death that Sean promised to take her back to Ireland, to try and make up for all the pain he had caused her in her life. If it hadn't been for Sean and some of his terrible decisions, maybe Kate would not have turned to alcohol. And if Kate had not turned to alcohol, she would in all likelihood still be alive.

Instead, her ashes were on a plane to Ireland. The night before Kate died, she had asked Sean to take her there after she passed and spread her ashes so that she could become part of that great country where her grandparents had been born and where she and Sean had started their marriage. Today, Sean was bringing his best friend home, and it hurt. The pain in his heart deepened as he considered how he had also lost the relationship with his children ever since Kate had died. This wasn't how things were supposed to go.

"Where will this trip take me?" Sean asked himself. His professional life had just changed dramatically, his personal life was a mess, and he had been struggling with his faith in God given everything that had happened over the past three years. The only part of his life that seemed to be in decent shape at all was his physical health. After Kate had passed, he started going to the gym again, returned to the game of golf, and even joined a running club. The irony that it was Kate who had told him for years he needed to take better care of himself and that he was only now exercising religiously after her passing was not lost on him. But Sean also couldn't help but feel that Kate just might be looking down on him from Heaven and smiling.

In the past when Kate and Sean would travel, it was Kate who would always make new friends where they went. Hopefully Sean would be able to meet some people through a rendezvous with the Hash House Harriers, an international running club that often frequents drinking establishments after a good run. Four weeks was a long time to travel alone. He had hoped some of his golfing buddies from back home would be able to join him on this trip but no one was able to make the trip on such short notice. Then again, Sean thought, "being alone may be the best thing for me." He had been mentoring people for years about the need to go someplace special when you are in the midst of challenge and crisis—now it was time to take his own advice.

The truth was that Sean needed to call a "time out" in his life to digest everything that had happened, not just since Kate's passing but since the recent travails at the hospital, which had forced him to resign. Then, of course, there was the question of, "What next?" Sean hoped in Ireland to begin to determine what he wanted to do with the rest of his life. He did not want to retire, and yet he knew the chances of someone hiring a 62-year-old hospital administrator were slim.

3

Go Down and In Before
Going Up and Out

Within a few short hours of landing in Ireland, Sean was checking into his hotel in Doolin, called the Aran View. It was a beautiful hotel overlooking the Arin Isle and the surrounding green countryside. As he signed his name in the guest book, Sean admitted to Sue Gay, the owner of the hotel, that the drive from the airport was a little challenging with trying to get used to driving on the "wrong side of the road."

"Just you wait," Sue warned. "On some roads, it will seem like big green hedges will be hitting the car on both sides and then up ahead you will see a sign that reads, ROAD NARROWS."

Sean thought, "Ah, Irish humor," and yet the visual of Sue's story made him think that driving throughout Ireland was going to take some getting used to.

* * *

After a run with the Hash House Harriers and a quick jaunt to the pub with his new friends, Sean walked back to the hotel. Along the way, he was struck by the sheer beauty of the town of Doolin and the Arin Isle. The homes were centuries old and well kept, the streets were clean, and the views of the Galway Bay were spectacular.

As he entered the Arin View, Sean walked through the lobby with its high wooden ceiling and high-back guest chairs where he was greeted by Sue Gay.

"You have a special delivery waiting for you in your room," she announced. "What on earth could it be?" Sean thought. He didn't expect to hear from anyone while on this trip.

Upon entering his room, Sean was taken aback by the volume of flowers, all native to Ireland, that were bursting from a large glass vase on the writing table. The card from the florist highlighted each type of flower, beginning with shell flowers, Easter lilies, amaryllis, and bright yellow roses. The card in the sealed envelope was from Maryanne Richmond, which said, "Thank you for believing in me. Enjoy your time away!"

Next to the flowers was a plate of recently baked, cranberry scones that also was from Maryanne who knew that Sean just loved his scones. Sean picked up his smart phone feeling the urge to send Maryanne an email or a text. But then he remembered something his Kate used to say whenever they went on vacation: "If you do not disconnect, you will never recharge." Easier said than done for a Type A personality.

Sean caved to the pressure and dropped Maryanne a quick line of thanks from his personal email account. (The Health System had wasted no time locking him out of the hospital email and voicemail systems.) As he hit the send button, his account automatically updated with new messages. There was only one that caught his attention, and he simply could not ignore it. It was from assistant Erin; she had forwarded an email with a subject line stating, "Thought you might find this message interesting."

The message attached was from Sister Elizabeth Seton (the Chairperson of the Holy Spirit Health System Board), announcing the hiring of a Patricia

Scott as the interim CEO for the Health System to replace Miles Greene. Through national health care circles, Sean knew of Pat Scott's reputation as someone who led with "an iron fist covered by a velvet glove." Pat was no stranger to Catholic healthcare and knew the importance of maintaining the Catholic identity while also being financially successful. She had recently retired from a large healthcare system in Long Island, New York, and appeared to be joining Holy Spirit on a temporary basis.

Sean thought, "The system Board must be serious about cleaning things up by bringing in someone with Pat's background and experience." Pat was known as a no-nonsense type of person who was not afraid to get her hands dirty in order to get things done. As Sean was closing the email down, he smiled, thinking, "One thing's for sure—Brown's not going to be happy with this development."

Maybe it was the good news that someone responsible was taking over the Health System or maybe it was the intense run with the Harriers followed by some dark Irish stout, but that night, Sean slept deeply.

He had set his alarm, so the following day he was up early so he could go to Sunday mass, just like at home. He attended the 10 AM service at the Holy Rosary Church, which he found quite enjoyable due to the small chapel and wonderful singing by everyone in attendance.

Then it was on to an early lunch and a round of golf at the Lahinch Golf Club Old Course. Sean played the round with three other locals who helped him find his way around the links-style course. Oftentimes during the round, the locals would say, "Thank your lucky stars the wind isn't blowing." Sean thought that was quite humorous since the wind was howling at a steady 30 mph right off the ocean; yet his playing mates felt it was a calm day.

After carding a round of 98, Sean felt okay with the results given the harsh conditions throughout the day and found his way to O'Connor's pub for an after-round pint or two. Doolin was known for its music, and O'Connor's pub was often the main meeting place for local musicians.

Since it was a Sunday evening, the crowd was light, which gave Sean a chance to chat with the regular weekend bartender. After introductions, the bartender began to ask Sean about his trip and learned of Sean's interest in playing golf. The bartender was an avid golfer, and he knew the Lahinch course very well, so he asked, "What was your favorite hole?" Sean went on to share how unique the course was compared to the courses back home.

"So give me an example," the bartender said.

"I could not find the damn fifth green," Sean replied. "It was surrounded by not large mounds but hills!"

The bartender responded, "Oh, that hole is named the 'Dell,'" to which Sean responded, "It might as well be called 'Hell' because I took an 8 on that par 3 hole." The bartender and some other regulars laughed.

Sean went on to add, "On the very next hole, I hit possibly the best drive of my life, only to find it at the bottom of a ten-foot-deep bomb crater in the middle of the sixth fairway." Just the way Sean explained the sixth hole and how he had a hard time getting out of the fairway bunker made the bartender bend over with laughter.

As Sean was waiting for another pint of Harp to be poured, he noticed an older gentleman sitting in the corner, smiling at Sean's golf stories. The old regular's name was Frank Hetherton, and he said to the bartender, "Put the lad's next beer on my tab for all of his troubles." Sean thanked Frank for the beer and struck up a conversation where he learned that Frank was eighty-one years old and originally from Westmeath, Ireland. Frank worked his whole career shoveling coal to support this wife of sixty years, Mamie, and their two sons. As it turned out, Frank used to caddie at the Lahinch Golf Course on weekends to make some extra money so he knew quite well of the problems Sean had experienced earlier in the day. The more they talked, the more Sean could sense there was more to Frank than met the eye.

Frank asked, "So what brings you to Ireland all by yourself other than to play some golf?" It was one of those questions that Sean knew carried a deeper meaning.

Sean responded, "Let's just say I have had some significant changes happening in my life right now, and I hope to get some answers while I am here in your beautiful country as to what to do next."

Frank listened for a bit, then looked Sean directly in the eye. "So you are at an intersection in your life, and you don't know what to do next and that scares the hell out of you?"

Sean was surprised by this last comment and thought, "How does this gentleman who I just met know so much about my struggles?" There was a long pause before Sean spoke. "Yes, that is exactly what I am doing here, and I hope and pray for some answers."

Frank stared straight out into some foreign space and finally said, "You came to the right place, but the answers will not come as easily as you would like. Are you ready to do the work?"

"I have never been afraid to work hard for anything I believe in," Sean replied.

Frank continued, "In order for you to go on with your life, you will have to go down and in before you can go back up and out. You will need to get to the core of who you are, what you believe in, and what you care about before you will be able to go on with the rest of your life. Only then will you be able to enjoy the rewards of the struggle."

As Sean processed Frank's comments, he felt like a fighter who had just been shocked by a hard punch to the jaw. He knew he would recover, but he was dazed for a moment. Sean was thankful Frank did not speak for a moment, which allowed him to regain his focus.

"I get the sense you have been successful in your previous life by working hard, but the work I am talking about will be unlike anything you have ever done before. For once in your life, you will have to do more listening than speaking. And remember this when you are saying your prayers like you were this morning at Mass: the prayers are not so God will hear you but more so that you will hear God."

* * *

As Sean walked back to the Arin View Hotel, past the cow pasture in a light mist, he pulled his hat low and his jacket collar up high as he was replaying the conversation with Frank Hetherton. Who was this local character? Then Sean remembered something the bartender had said as Sean was leaving the pub. "Frank does not usually speak to many strangers so I suggest you take his words to heart. The locals have been going to him for years for advice and he is rarely wrong." The final thought Sean took away from his conversation with Frank was an old saying he heard years ago: "When the student is ready, the teacher will appear." Sean laughed to himself, thinking, "I wonder if old Frank will come back to Chicago with me."

4

God's Anonymous Ways

As Sean was sitting in church on Thursday morning thinking about the past three weeks, he began to realize how he was finally starting to unwind and feel relaxed. The tenseness in his shoulders was gone at last, and his ability to sleep soundly through the night had returned to like it was when he was in his twenties. The freedom to come and go as he pleased was very different from his former executive life where it seemed every minute was scheduled, sometimes even double and tripled scheduled. The time in this rich, green, and rustic country was just what he needed in order to finally "work on himself."

A few days ago, while walking the County Sligo Golf Course alone, Sean decided he needed to begin to get different parts of his life back in balance. His physical life was fine, but the professional, personal, mental, and spiritual parts of his life were largely out of synch. Realizing that all four parts were not going to come back at once, Sean decided to begin by focusing on the spiritual part. This is why he started to attend daily Mass and spend some quiet time alone in the local church.

On this particular day, while Sean was walking throughout Holy Rosary Church, he noticed how he no longer felt like he had to be praying the whole time and that he could just let his mind go free in an effort to listen to what God was telling him. While walking, Sean observed the beauty in the old stain glass windows and the detail in the hand-carved alter rail. Both items had been here the whole time, and yet it wasn't until now that Sean "saw" them for the first time.

As Sean continued to walk, he could not help but remember the words of Frank Hetherton, who had said that Sean would have to go "down and in" before he could "go back up and out." Sean understood Frank's point that we all need a strong foundation on which to build our lives before we can go out into the world to make our mark. Just like he observed for the first time the intrinsic beauty of the church, Sean was beginning to gain some personal insights that would help him repair the cracks in his own foundation.

Over the past week or so, there were times that Sean seemed to lose track of the hours while spending time in Holy Rosary Church. On this particular day, while sitting in one of the church pews, Sean spent time thinking about his career and family. He finally admitted to himself that he had been married to his job for years, charging hard and glad-handing people over too many drinks. He had lost his perspective on the importance of his family—though Kate never did. She always worked hard to balance everything out.

Sean looked up to God and thought guiltily, "Kate would always support me in front of Timothy and Katherine when they asked why I was not around, saying 'Your father has a very important job that requires him to spend a great amount of time at work.' But you know just as well as me Lord that because of this, I missed a great deal of the children's formative years, with me working those sixty- and seventy-hour weeks and being out many weeknights at work-related functions."

Sean thought about how Kate would volunteer to attend as many work functions as she could so she could be near Sean when he was available; the rest of the time she would tend to their children and take care of things at home. "Laundry and lunch boxes" she used to say with a smile. As Sean stood after kneeling for quite some time, his knees ached and so did his heart upon realizing how many things he had missed during his children's youth.

Sean continued to tell his thoughts to God, saying, "In spite of my missing so much time, the children worshiped me and it was all due to the support Kate provided while I was not at home. To my credit I did learn how to make each child feel special when I was with them, which helped to keep me in good standing in their young eyes. Whether it was a special present or an unexpected trip to the ice cream store, small gestures like these always made me seem like a hero in Timothy and Katherine's eyes."

Sean was jostled out of his thoughts by the sounds of the priest getting ready for afternoon confessions. As he broke from his prayer and contemplation, Sean was shocked to see that almost three hours had gone by since he had first arrived at the church. He stood up, stretched his legs, and turned to go. As Sean walked out of the church, he was greeted by Frank Hetherton, who Sean could now see was a rather frail man weighing no more than 120 pounds. The years of shoveling coal had taken its toll on his body and his lungs. It wasn't until last week that Sean learned that Frank was the sexton of the Holy Rosary church and that was how Frank had known about Sean visiting the church when they first met almost three weeks ago. Frank just smiled and said, "I didn't think you were ever coming out." This made Sean laugh, before he went on to accept Frank's invitation to sit down on a bench just outside the church.

"So have any of our other golf courses kicked your arse lately?" Frank asked.

Sean remembered the night in O'Connor's Pub when he first met Frank. Since then, Sean had often replayed in his mind their conversation about the work Sean would need to do in order to decide which path of "the intersection" he would take. Would he really retire or would he continue working?

Frank let some time pass and then asked, "So what have you learned about yourself since that night at O'Connor's Pub?"

"Well," Sean replied, "the foundation on which I am built has some cracks due to some of my recent life experiences, and yet I am beginning to feel that those cracks are reparable."

Frank said, "Well, that sure is some improvement."

"But you know, Frank," Sean acknowledged, "I am still really angry with God about the death of my wife and the way my relationship with my kids has fallen apart. Throw in my recent firing from work and I am feeling quite bitter."

Frank said, "We do not have enough time today to discuss all of those areas so why not just pick the one you feel is most important." With that invitation, Sean just launched into sharing things about his family. He began by telling Frank everything he had just been thinking about in church—the way he had been married to his job and had not dedicated enough time to loving and taking care of his wife and children. He also explained how Kate had done a good job for a long time in keeping up with him, attending work social events, cocktails and all.

"Eventually, though, things began to change," Sean explained to Frank. "As the children got older, Kate's drinking started to get out of control. I thought it was okay—or maybe I just wanted it to be okay—until one day when the children were both in high school. They waited up for me one night while Kate was sleeping and shared with me their concern about her drinking."

Sean could remember the moment as if it was yesterday. He continued, "They told me that Kate would start to drink in the early afternoon, and they would often find her slurring her words when they arrived home from school. I told them everything was okay and they didn't need to worry—but I was just trying to protect them. I knew then that something was wrong."

Frank raised his hand so as to signal to Sean he needed a break to say hello to some of the parishioners as they were making their way into church for confessions.

After a moment, Sean continued, "After that night, I began to notice how Kate's drinking was truly spiraling out of control. At the same time, I started to realize that the children were pulling away from me. I chose to deal with it by spending more time at work and hoping everything would be okay. But it wasn't."

Frank added, "Married to your work, were you? The curse of many successful people who feel they need to put in long hours in order to be successful."

"Several months later, Kate admitted that she had totally lost control. All she could think about when she woke up in the morning was when and where she'd get her next drink. She had started mixing Bailey's in her morning coffee! She was drinking vodka tonics with lunch."

"Because of my stature in the community, we had her go to an alcohol treatment facility in Maryland. It was during that time while Kate was away that I decided to stop drinking in order to support Kate when she came home. Since her death, I will occasionally have a pint or two but nowhere near the amount I used to drink. For Kate, there were several years of sobriety followed by a few relapses. Kate died three years ago from the complications associated with alcoholism and I have not forgiven myself ever since."

The tears were running down Sean's face when he finished, and finally Frank spoke. He asked Sean, "Did your wife forgive you while she was alive?" Sean thought for a moment, and as he began to answer, the tears began to flow. "Yes, my Kate said many times that she forgave me for whatever wrongs I had done."

Frank picked up on this last comment and added, "So your wife has forgiven you, but you as of yet have not forgiven yourself? So maybe instead of being angry at God for everything that has happened recently, you are really angry at yourself. I can tell you from experience that your true healing will come once you begin to forgive yourself."

Sean remembered Frank's comment earlier about going "down and in" and felt like he just hit the bottom of his own deep place. Frank could sense Sean was processing all that was just said and added, "So think about how you want your legacy to be remembered and begin to chart your new course. God still has plans for you; just remain open to whatever comes your way."

Sean sat there because he was stunned once again by Frank's wisdom. "There is no such thing in life as a coincidence," a grade school nun had once told Sean, *"only God acting anonymously."* Through some divine intervention or maybe it was through the intercession of Kate, Sean had been brought to Ireland to meet this wise old man. When he finally could comprehend all that Frank had just said, Sean asked, "Where do I begin?"

Frank said, "That's easy. Go around to the rectory and ask Father Conor Lenahan to hear your confession. Swallow your pride, confess all of your sins, ask for forgiveness, and be open to whatever God has in store for you. Father Lenahan listens really well, and he will give you more insights than I just did. Oh and be prepared, Father Lenahan has a tendency to go on for quite a bit, but he gives really easy penance."

* * *

On his last full day in Ireland, Sean took a road trip to the small town of Connemara, in County Galway. It was there that he would spread Kate's ashes. Even though there was an official Catholic burial service for Kate five days after her death including a headstone in Chicago, Sean knew he would quietly honor Kate's wishes to scatter her ashes in Ireland.

On their honeymoon visit there, Kate had once said that Connemara was the most beautiful place on earth. During their engagement, when discussing the honeymoon, Kate had said, "You can take me anywhere, but it must include a stop in Connemara so I can see and smell the flowers where Maureen O'Hara ran through the beautiful countryside." She was referring to one of her favorite scenes from the John Wayne movie, "The Quiet Man." They had made it to Connemara on their honeymoon, and now Sean was here to bring his bride home to rest in eternal peace.

Sean found a beautiful, quiet place right beside a small babbling brook where he decided to scatter Kate's ashes. Sean happened to notice that some of the flowers in the meadow were the same that were in the flower arrangement that Maryanne had sent the first day he arrived. This realization sent a chill down Sean's spine. As he began to unscrew the lid of the urn containing Katie's ashes, his eyes began to fill with tears of loss. He was comforted by the thought that he was bringing Kate to a place on this earth that she loved and had wanted to be part of for all eternity. Sean was also thankful for the most recent conversation with Frank Hetherton and for the confession with Father Lenahan because he had less guilt and fear than he thought he would at this moment. He now believed that God had forgiven him for all of the pain he had caused Kate; he was also beginning to forgive himself.

Before turning the urn over to release Kate's ashes, Sean said with a full-throated voice, "My dear Kate, please forgive me and know I will always love you." As Sean was beginning to tilt the urn, a strong gust of wind came and helped to carry Kate's ashes far and wide. "Okay, God. So what plans do you have in store for me now?"

5

THUNDER ROAD

THE FLIGHT HOME from Ireland was two hours late arriving in Chicago due to a weather delay in getting out of Ireland. Normally, such a delay would have driven Sean crazy, but not now. This was a positive sign that his walkabout had helped him to decompress and relax. The old Sean would have been uptight the whole plane ride home and probably needed several scotch and waters to calm him down. On this flight, Sean would not need anything but the airplane pillow and his new book about golf titled *A Course Called Ireland*.

While in the air, Sean had a chance to replay his trip from beginning to end. He was able to play fourteen rounds of golf on some of the most challenging and beautiful courses in the world. He stayed at some of the most comfortable hotels, none better than the Arin View Hotel. And he met some amazing people, including Frank Heatherton and Sue Gay.

The friendship with Frank had ended as it began with the local bartender pouring Sean one last pint of Harp while Frank enjoyed a pint of Guinness. Sean thanked Frank for everything he had said and done during their time together. Frank said in a rather insightful way, "I have done nothing if you do not do something with what I said."

Most important, Sean was able to spread Kate's ashes in Connemara. The beauty of the brook where Sean left Kate's ashes would always be one of the fondest memories he would have of Ireland. Kate was finally "at home" and Sean had begun to find peace within himself, his relationship with God, and whatever lay ahead for his life and his career.

Sean opted not to watch a movie on the flight home, choosing instead to remain introspective while glancing through his new book. As he turned its pages, something in him clicked, and he decided he was going to continue on with his career, not knowing where or in what capacity. Though he was initially worried as to who would hire a 62-year-old former hospital CEO, he was reminded of an old Neil Young song that said, "It is better to burn out than to rust out."

"Retirement is not for me," Sean thought, "and now I must find my next opportunity." Sean also thought, "Thank God for faith because the old me would never have been so comfortable with such unknowns."

* * *

Sean was home for just thirty minutes when there was a knock on his front door.

"Who the hell can that be? Who even knows I am home?" Sean wondered. With that, he looked through the peephole and could see standing at his front door none other than Luther Jackson, his old friend from Divine Mercy Hospital. Luther had been on the Chicago police force for twenty-one years before his accident. He was injured saving a child from a car fire, which resulted in a broken leg and burns to 30% of his lower body. Luther was taken to Divine Mercy Hospital when he was injured and spent the next three months recovering in the hospital's burn unit. It was during that time that Sean met Luther while making rounds one day and that Sean made it a point to stop by and visit every time he was out circulating the hospital.

It was during one of Sean's visits that he learned of Luther's concern about getting his job back and his ability to care for his wife, son, and daughter, who was recently diagnosed with multiple sclerosis. Sean made Luther a promise in that if he could not get his job back on the Chicago Police force, then Divine Mercy would hire him to be part of the hospital security department. Six weeks after being discharged from the hospital, Luther began his job as Assistant Supervisor in the Divine Mercy Security Department.

As Sean opened the door and gave Luther a big hug, he was impressed with how solid Luther felt and how in shape he was for a 54-year-old guy. After Luther's accident, he had recommitted himself to getting back in and remaining in great physical condition.

Sean asked, "What brings you here?" and Luther handed Sean his mail and said, "I wanted to make sure you got all of your love mail as soon as you got home."

Sean then asked, "How are my Cubbies doing?" to which Luther gave Sean a quick update on his favorite baseball team. Sean added, "So nothing has changed since I left. We're still in last place." They both just smiled since being a lifelong Cub's fan meant you had to have a sense of humor.

After some thirty minutes of getting caught up on most of the highlights of Sean's travels, Luther gave Sean an update on how he'd been over the last month and added how his son was holding his own while fighting that "son of a bitch disease." Luther's son was an alcoholic, and Sean had been very supportive of Luther trying to help him.

"There's another reason why I'm here," Luther confessed.

Sean laughed and said, "What? To offer my old job back?" Sean added that he had decided while he was away not to retire even if he wasn't quite sure what was next for him. "Let's just say I have a renewed interest in blind faith," Sean said, "which is very uncommon for a CEO. The trip took me to places I did not expect but at the same time helped me to see certain things more clearly."

After a pause, Luther blurted, "The new System CEO, Pat Scott, wants to meet with you as soon as possible." Talk about a bolt of lightning out of nowhere.

"Huh?" Sean asked in disbelief.

"That's all I know," Luther said, "but I do know it must be important if they sent me over here on your first day back."

Sean let what Luther had just said sink in and then asked, "How did the brand new system CEO even know what my plans were and how to get a hold of me?" Luther just smiled and said, "Your former Executive Assistant could only hold out for so long, and I understand from talking to Erin that the 'new boss lady' can be very persuasive. Scott also asked that Erin reach out to you in a way that would not draw any unusual attention, hence Erin called me to be the messenger." Sean just laughed and figured he would eventually get the real scoop on what happened from Erin herself.

Luther reported, "Pat has hit the ground running and is not making many decisions yet but is sure as hell asking a lot of questions."

Luther asked Sean what he knew about Pat, and Sean responded, "Not much other than that she has turned around other failing health systems and recently decided to retire. I also seem to remember reading that she was working with a federal tort reform bill that would help all providers. If she has signed on to help our System, there must have been some strong connection to talk her out of her recent retirement. The Board must sense their problems run pretty deep to bring in someone of Scott's experience to fill the interim role."

"My belief," Sean continued, "is that the Board will only seek an outsider for one of four reasons: to initiate a financial turnaround, to reestablish credibility, to develop a new culture, and finally to implement a new strategic direction for the organization. My guess is that Pat has been given her marching orders to complete a thorough evaluation of all four areas so the Board will know what type of skill sets to seek in the next permanent CEO for the Health system."

As Luther listened to Sean speak about leadership, he only wished there could be a role for Sean at the Health System in the future, knowing that it was Sean's type of leadership that was needed there. "Fat chance that will happen since they ran Sean out of here less than two months ago," Luther thought. "Oh, but one can dream."

After Sean said goodbye to Luther, Sean spent the next hour going through his mail. He found two letters of interest. One was from a recruiting firm asking whether he was interested in a small health system CEO role in South Bend, Indiana, and the other was from a large academic teaching hospital in New York inquiring if he was interested in an open CEO position.

Holding these letters in his hand, he remembered how just a short time ago he had gotten out of a car and was standing on his porch wondering what vehicle for change was around the bend in the road. This visual reminded Sean of a line from one of his favorite Bruce Springsteen songs, "Thunder Road," which said, "From your front porch to my front seat, the door is open but the ride ain't free." Sean felt like the earth had moved a little bit with the news that Pat Scott wanted to meet with him. The question was, what would come of this meeting because he knew the ride was not going to be free.

6

ARE YOU KIDDING ME?

S EAN CALLED PAT Scott's cell phone on Sunday as was suggested in the handwritten note he received via Luther. Sean found Pat to be quite cordial over the phone. She was even interested to learn about his trip to Ireland and the life experiences he had during his time away. They spoke for almost an hour. At the very end of the call, they made plans to meet Monday morning.

After Sean hung up, he was struck by the leadership style of Pat and how she seemed truly interested in Sean the person, not just Sean the former CEO of Divine Mercy Hospital. It was a drastic change compared to the leadership style of Miles Greene. Greene never asked about anything in Sean's personal life because he was strictly business. In fact, Sean could not remember Greene ever asking about Kate, especially when she was sick except for that one call when Greene threatened to make information about Kate's alcoholism public to the Board unless Sean gave into a request made by Charles Brown. Sean could remember that day and that call as if it had just happened.

Sean selected a location along Lake Shore drive as a place to meet since the

Chicago August weather was forecasted to be unusually pleasant. The specific directions were to meet at a brightly painted, yellow bench located on a small bend in the road by the Drake Hotel. This was a spot where Sean still had many good memories of when he and Kate were newlyweds and they used to ride bikes along the lake for fun since they had no money for anything else. Sean also thought this would be an easy place for Pat to find given that she was new to town.

Sean was surprised when Scott came up and introduced herself.

"How did you know who I was?" Sean asked.

"By the description provided by Erin," she replied.

Sean asked, "How did my loyal former assistant describe me to you?" Pat chuckled and said, "Look for a short fellow who will be wearing long khaki pants, a new golf shirt, and brown casual boat shoes." As Pat finished with the description provided by Erin, she added, "I couldn't have missed you if I tried."

All Sean could do was grin because Erin had described him exactly as he was dressed for this meeting, down to the new shirt from the Lahinch Golf Club. Sean thought, "Oh Erin, you know me better than I know myself. You were one of the first employees I hired sixteen years ago and you have stayed with me through the good, the bad, and the ugly."

"Whatever you were paying Erin, it surely was not enough," Pat said. They both laughed at that last statement.

As they started walking, Pat began to redirect the conversation by asking, "Did you come to any new career insights while in Ireland, or are you going to stay retired?"

"Well," Sean explained, "I met this elderly gentleman who made me think about who I am and what I want to do next. And along the way I discovered that I want to continue to work in an executive role but I am just not sure what is the right role or opportunity."

Now it was Sean's turn to ask a direct question: "Who do you know that could coax you out of retirement to take on the interim assignment for the Health System?"

Pat laughed and said, "The provincial for the sponsoring religious order who 'owns' the Health System. The good Sister is an old friend and someone who I could not say no to for all she has done for me and my career."

Sean seemed satisfied and went on to ask his second question: "What is a Long Islander doing in the land of the Chicago Cubs and Bears territory?" After Sean had spoken to Pat on Sunday, he had done some research on Pat's background and learned that she was born and raised in Rockaway Beach, Queens, New York. From there, Sean just assumed Pat was either a Mets or Yankees fan or either a Jets or Giants fan. As it turned out, Pat was a Mets and a Jets fan, though she promised to keep an open mind about Chicago sports.

Pat then asked, "Can I be direct with you?"

Sean said, "Yes, and that would be a welcome change given the history of our Health System's culture."

Pat went on to say that even though she had only been on the job for a few weeks, she was beginning to think that the Health System was in serious trouble on several fronts. "First, the finances appear to not be as good as have been reported. Second, I believe the System is not producing the type of quality outcomes that will be needed to succeed under the Accountable Care Act." She went on to add, "But that is the least of our problems. Third and most important to me and for the long-term success of the Health System, I believe we have a serious succession-planning problem, and no one seems concerned about it from what I can tell. The people who appear to be in the wings to take over for some on the planned retirements do not have the business and leadership skills needed to succeed in Healthcare Reform."

This last point did not surprise Sean, and he added, "I shared that very similar concern with both Miles Greene and Steve Driver but to no avail."

Pat continued, "Once in my career, I was a CEO for a health system that had seven hospitals. Soon after I became CEO, I learned that the real reason for the poor financial performance was that those seven hospitals had had twenty-two CEO changes in the previous five years. The negative impact of all that CEO turnover was the underlying reason for the poor financial, strategic, and quality performance."

As Pat paused, Sean asked, "So let me ask again, now that you've had some time to get to know the Health System here, why did you accept this position?"

Pat chuckled and said, "I knew I was getting into a turnaround situation, but I didn't know it was going to be this bad. The real challenge for us today is to try and find a way to fix all of these areas and not have the press find out about the degree of our deficiencies, or all Hell will break lose around here. Believe me, a media circus will make our job of turning around this System that much harder."

As Sean was listening to Pat, he was thinking how this woman really knew her stuff and how she was also a quick study of how this system had operated for years. Sean had long been frustrated by the pressure the Health System leaders would put on him and the other hospital CEOs to produce better financial and quality results. Sean in particular was on the receiving end of extra pressure because his hospital was financially stronger than the other hospitals, As a result, Sean used to work hard to hide some profits on the balance sheet to act as a "rainy day" fund in case there was an off year or for when an unexpected adjustment needed to be made. The Health System found out about these efforts with the help of the outside auditing firm.

This resulted in the books for Divine Mercy being scrutinized even closer to make sure Sean was not hiding anything that could make the bottom line look better. This really pissed Sean off, but he learned on some things that he just had to "go along to get along." He felt there were other more important battles to fight.

Sean was pleased with the place he had selected to meet Pat since it turned out to be such a nice summer day. They had left the Lake Shore Drive area and were now walking along the famous Magnificent Mile in downtown Chicago. Because Sean was a native to this area, he did not even notice the 26-foot statue of Marilyn Monroe. Pat stopped and said to Sean, "I have never heard of or seen anything like that statue. How long has it been here?" Sean shared that it arrived in July 2011 and would be here for a while longer before moving on to Palm Springs, CA. The statue was a depiction of the famous photo from the 1955 movie called the "Seven Year Itch" where Monroe's dress goes flying as she is standing over a subway grate. Pat asked about how it had been received, and Sean said, "Ah, it is mainly a tourist attraction, but it's fun to watch the men stand next to their wives or girlfriends under the statue for a picture and try not to look up."

Pat chuckled. "Men, you are all alike."

Sean just kept on walking and said, "It isn't easy being a guy these days," which drew a big laugh from Pat.

As they walked past the statue, Pat continued, "Like I said, I am most concerned with the lack of succession planning and leadership development across the entire system. I estimate that in the next five to seven years, the system could have eight to ten key positions turn over due to just retirements. This does not take into account leaders who will leave once the new CEO comes in and wants to put his or her own team together. Once a new CEO comes in within eighteen months of starting the job, approximately 50% of the existing executive team will turn over. Because of this need, I believe we should start immediately with developing a system-wide Succession and Leadership Development Plan."

Sean raised his hand as if asking for permission to speak, and as Pat paused he added, "I was aware of the high cost of CEO turnover but not that 50% of the executive team would also turn over soon after the new CEO was hired."

"It's extreme but true," Pat replied.

"Now, you may wonder why I wanted to meet with you and how my sharing with you my impressions of the Health System may impact you?" Pat continued. "First, I have been impressed with Maryanne Richmond as she has settled into her new role as CEO of your former hospital. When I met with her, she kept on singing your praises for having mentored and developed her so that she was ready when you left."

"How is Charles Brown treating Maryanne?" Sean asked.

"Brown's trying to intimidate Maryanne, but she seems to be holding her ground," Pat replied.

"I never should have let that slimy politician on to the hospital Board," Sean interjected.

Pat knew there must be more to that story, but she decided to let it be and return to her comments related to Sean. Pat started back up by saying, "Second, the general consensus among many of the people I have interviewed is that you are really missed by a great majority of the people. Several of those I interviewed mentioned how you finally must have pushed the wrong buttons and that Greene finally decided to take you out with a significant assistance from Charles Brown." Sean was smiling at what Pat was saying because he agreed with her conclusion about his departure, but while in Ireland Sean had also decided to move forward and not dwell on the past.

Pat's tone changed when she said, "I can't give you your old job back, but I'm wondering if you would consider helping me out?"

"What do you have in mind?" Sean replied.

"I want you to come back and help develop a system-wide Succession and Leadership Development Plan. I want you to do for the Health System what you did at your hospital." Pat was referring to Sean's mentoring and development of the next generation of leaders during his tenure at Divine Mercy. Upon hearing Pat's invitation, Sean thought back to his trip to Ireland and how he had to talk himself into being open to whatever came next. His next reaction was mixed because on one hand he was initially excited to be in demand but on the other hand he was not sure if he wanted to give up on his being a hospital CEO. What's more, he wasn't too keen on working around the remaining three members of the Liars Club once again.

As they continued to walk along Michigan Avenue, Sean stopped and bent down to pick up a well-worn penny that was on the sidewalk. He did this without saying a word and, after looking at the date on the penny, pulled out his rosary case and placed the penny in there for safekeeping. Pat just watched Sean and finally asked, "Is finding old pennies a habit of yours?"

Sean just smiled and said, "Just something our family has done over the years."

"If you're interested, Sean, I would like you to start as soon as possible. I'm planning on having you report directly to Steve Driver, the CHRO for the Health System."

This last sentence caused Sean to stop in the middle of Michigan Avenue and state quite loudly, "I am not a fan of Steve Driver, and he does not like me very much either." In realizing that he would have to report to someone he did not trust nor respect—one of the perennial members of the Liars Club—Sean felt his initial excitement drain out of him. Sean felt that Driver was a weak CHRO who relied too heavily on outside consultants to complete his work. Because most of the work he produced came from a select number of consultants he relied on heavily, Driver did not have any internal credibility.

The second reason Sean did not like Driver's use of outside consultants is because it was Divine Mercy and the other hospitals that paid the fees charged by the consultants. This last part often angered Sean because most of the time Sean felt that the consultants' reports and recommendations were of little value. The bottom line was that nothing ever got done when Driver was involved unless the work was completed by some high-priced outsiders.

Sean thought for a moment and then responded. "I am flattered by your offer, Pat, but I'll have to think about it. I'm still trying to decide what to do with the next stage of my career. In fact, in the mail this weekend there were two recruiting letters from prestigious health care organizations asking about my interest in their vacant CEO positions. Even if I am interested in this job, the reporting relationship to Driver would be a problem for me."

Pat listened to what Sean had to say, and after a few seconds added, "The Health System has a significant need to develop a Succession and Leadership Plan, and I believe you're the person for the job. Related to your concern about reporting to Driver, I'm not sure I can make any change there. As the interim CEO, I'm hesitant to begin changing reporting relationships that may change again once the new CEO is in place. So I suppose where at a bit of an impasse."

As Sean hailed a cab to take Pat back to the Health System offices, she said, "I enjoyed meeting you, and I'm confident you can do an excellent job with developing the Succession and Leadership Development Plans for the Health System. But obviously you have to be on board with the move. Are you Sean?" she asked rhetorically and then continued, "I'll need your answer by Friday." With that, Pat ducked into the cab and became lost in her smart phone.

As the cab pulled away, Sean was left standing on the corner, realizing that he had a lot to think about before giving Pat an answer in a few days.

7

NEVER COMPROMISE YOUR VALUES

S EAN SPENT MONDAY and Tuesday thinking about the meeting with
Pat Scott while also settling back into daily "retired life" in his home
city of Chicago. Sean loved this city, and he loved the people that
grew up and stayed there. The work ethic was solid, and the people were loyal
to each other and particularly their sports teams. For football, they loved "Da
Bears." For basketball, many still wore original Michael Jordan gear in support of the Bulls. The Blackhawks were the popular hockey team with a rich
history of players like Stan Mikita, Tony Esposito, and Denis Savard. But
when it came to baseball, the fans had a choice between the White Sox and
the Cubs.

Since Sean grew up in Roscoe Village, he and his family had always
been Cubs fans. In his youth Sean would sometimes skip high school and
sneak into Wrigley Field to watch his beloved Cubbies. Kate was from the
Central Lakeview section of the North side, which to locals was also known
as Wrigleyville. Kate's father used to be an usher at the Cubs' weekend home
games, and her mom used to help clean up the stadium after games. Kate

and Sean's first date, in fact, was to a Cubs game at Wrigley Field. The game was played on July 6, 1974 against the Atlanta Braves. The Braves won 3-2, but the Cubs' loss was made a little easier due to the post-game, fourth of July fireworks. Kate was a big fan of the Cubs as well as fireworks, and Sean thought this would be one way for them both to remember their first date. Later, Sean learned from Kate that she loved their first date because she felt he was a real gentleman and she felt safe to be with him.

For most of their married years, Kate and Sean had Cubs season tickets. As Sean's career progressed, their season tickets got better. After their second child was born, they found four seats all together in Row 3, right behind third base. These were great seats that got them close to the action where they could even hear the infielders chatting with one another. This also presented somewhat of a problem, though, when they brought their children, Katherine and Timothy, to a game. The problem with having those seats along the third base line was that they all had to pay attention because foul balls were often hit right into their section. In fact, between Kate and Sean, they had collected seventeen foul balls over the thirty-two years as season ticket holders. Sean used to get upset with Kate because with every foul ball they caught, Kate would always want to give it away to some child. They finally worked out a deal that if their two children were at the game, they would get to keep the foul ball. If their children were not at the game, Kate would be allowed to give the foul ball away as long as it was not hit by one of Sean's favorite players, like Ernie Banks, Ron Santo, or Ryan Sandberg.

Sean and the family always had a fun time at the games and had made some life-long friends while attending them. In fact, there were many times that Sean would take the two children to a game, and those times had become some of the children's favorite memories with their father.

Since Kate's death three years ago, though, Sean had only attended about five home games a year. The memories were just too strong of all the good times both he and Kate had had there so he mostly stayed away. Plus, since the blow-up with his children, they had no interest in attending a game with their father; going to a game solo was often just a reminder to Sean of the family he had once had.

Still, Sean loved his Cubbies and couldn't completely stay away. He was pleased to learn the team had a night home game this Wednesday. He decided to go to the game to "disconnect for a while" given that he had spent the last sixty hours mulling over Pat's offer to take on a new role at the hospital system, as well as the other two job offers. Since Sean had not been attending a majority of Cubs home games, he had given the tickets to the Divine Mercy Employee Activity Committee to give out to employees and their family members as a reward for doing exceptional work. So Sean bought a general admission ticket and found a seat in the left-center-field bleachers. The Cubs were playing the Philadelphia Phillies and the Phillies were currently in first place. Sean thought about how hot it was earlier in the day, but now the night had cooled and it was a beautiful time to watch a game.

As the game entered the middle innings, Sean found himself thinking about the discussion he had had with Pat Scott on Monday. He had to admit he was intrigued by the offer, and yet he was struggling with whether to accept it. First, he was not sure which career move he really wanted to make next, other than knowing that he was not ready to retire. Should he relocate and take another CEO position, or take a less stressful position and try something different? Second, Sean was getting more excited about the position Pat Scott offered, but he knew he could not report into someone he didn't respect. If he had to report to Steve Driver, then that was a deal breaker. As he continued to think about what to do with his next career move, Sean heard a familiar voice that appeared to be calling out his name. It was like he was in a light sleep when he recognized the person calling his name was Sadie Norman.

When Sean finally realized it was Sadie, he smiled.

She said, "What are you doing up in the cheap seats? I thought you had seats right behind third base." Sean was sitting five seats in from the end of the aisles so he got up and walked over to where he could speak to Sadie without yelling past other fans who wanted to enjoy the game. Sean hugged Sadie, which was his trademark greeting with many of the employees from Divine Mercy. Sadie worked as an usher helping people find their seats for every home game. Sean had learned over the years that his employees "didn't care how much he knew until they knew how much he cared." Sean had also learned that the more he took interest in the employees outside of work, the more they seemed to care about the overall success of the hospital. Sadie had been with the hospital for twenty-three years and was there when things were bad, before they turned around. At first, Sadie used to give Sean and anyone in the executive ranks a hard time, but over time she had become a huge fan of Sean and "her" Divine Mercy.

As Sadie and Sean walked back up to the concourse area where they could chat without blocking the view of the other fans, Sean said, "Since Kate's death I've found it hard to sit in our old seats. So sometimes I just like to come out and sit in the bleachers and enjoy the game."

Sadie responded, "Enjoy the game? Mr. Sean, you were miles away from the game just now. I must have called your name five to six times before you heard me, and you know I have a loud voice." Sean laughed at that last comment because Sadie worked in the hospital cafeteria, and whenever Sean would come in to have lunch Sadie would bellow, "Mr. Sean is in the house." They would always banter back and forth in a very respectful way. In fact, it was Sadie who made sure that when Kate was hospitalized that someone took up a dinner tray so Sean would get something to eat.

Sean thought for few seconds and said to Sadie, "So it was that obvious that I was distracted?"

Sadie responded, "Distracted, Mr. Sean? You were so far away, you were on another planet. I been keeping my eye on you for a while, and you haven't touched your hotdog or your Old Style beer. What has gotten you so distracted when you are supposed to be retired?"

Sean admitted to Sadie that he had been thinking about what to do with the rest of his career and that he was not used to being in this position. "I feel somewhat lost about what to do next, and I'm really struggling with this decision."

Sadie laughed and said, "If I had just retired, I would be sitting right where you are now and enjoying *life* and my ice cold Old Style beer." Sean could picture Sadie sitting in the Wrigley bleachers doing just what she said and having a good old time.

"Sadie," Sean added, "I'm just not ready to retire. I feel I have more to offer, and yet I'm not sure I know what to do. In fact, the new system boss, Pat Scott, asked me if I want to come back and help develop our future leaders. On the surface that sounds like it could be exciting, but at the same time I feel scared because this will be a whole new assignment for me, very different from being a CEO. Plus, I'd have to report to Steve Driver." At first, Sean was surprised at how easy it was to say what he had just said to Sadie and then at the same time he hoped he had not said too much. Sean was reminded how since Kate was gone he had no one to talk to about some of these life challenges.

Sadie got a little animated and said, "Mr. Sean, we would love for you to come back and help us out. In fact, some of the employees are beginning to think the Health System is in trouble and that having you back would certainly help. Mr. Sean, people trust you and believe in you, and if you come back, many of the employees would feel a whole lot better. But as for you reporting into that goofball Driver, 'Hell no' would be my answer. There is no way you should report to someone as weak as Driver; you could run circles around him."

Before Sean could continue thinking about what Sadie had just said about Driver, she interrupted: "And one more thing about that Driver dude. Whenever he came into the cafeteria at our hospital, he never said hello or nothing. Hell, he was the head of the entire Human Resources Department for our System and yet he never would give us employees the time of day."

As Sean thought about what Sadie had said, he asked, "Why do the employees feel the Health System is in trouble?"

"Oh Mr. Sean, you know how we all talk. My 'peeps' that work at the Health System office tell me this new Miss CEO Scott is asking a whole bunch of questions that are making everyone nervous. She's having those stuffed shirts working their asses off, and I hear 'on the drum' that they do not like it. Sometimes, we employees know a whole bunch more than you bosses give us credit for."

Something Sadie said made Sean think about a favorite saying from his high school baseball coach: "We will not change until the pain level gets high enough." Sean was trying to figure out if the pain he had experienced over the last few years as a hospital CEO was enough to get him to now move into a role like the one proposed by Pat Scott, which could truly help the Health System stabilize over the long-term. The role Scott proposed would not have all of the pressures of his old job, and yet he would have a chance to do what he loved—develop new leaders. Remembering the high school lesson about pain also made Sean think about what Father Lenahan had said while in confession: 'It is through the pain in life that we grow and arrive at a new place. We just have to be open to where the new opportunity will come and then be willing to say 'yes.'"

Sean's mind was racing with a thought, "Did I just decide to take this new role that Pat Scott proposed?" when he began to refocus again and heard Sadie's voice. "Mr. Sean, there you go again, off to some distant place. The last thing I will say is, listen to your heart and to God and you will make the right decision."

Sean thought, "Sadie, from your lips to God's ears."

Sadie then asked, "How are your two babies doing?" which jolted Sean out of thinking about himself and reminded him about how quickly things had deteriorated with Timothy and Katherine since Kate had died. He knew he had to repair their broken relationship but the time was just not right.

Sean hoped Sadie did not see the look of hurt on his face when he answered, "Oh Sadie, thanks for asking. They are both fine and moving ahead with their young lives. It's hard to believe Timothy is thirty-three and Katherine is thirty years old. It was great to see you, and please tell all of my friends back at the hospital I miss them. Also, please keep our little discussion confidential until I make my decision." As Sadie turned to go back to work, she added, "Don't worry, Baby, our little conversation will stay between you and I."

After the game, which the Phillies won 8-7 when Chase Utley hit a two-run homerun in the ninth inning, Sean was on the Red line train heading home and replaying his thoughts and conversation with Sadie. He smiled when he realized that he had actually had fun at the game; he decided to get back to attending more of them, like he used to. It was initially hard to be there without Kate, but he found the confines of Wrigley Field to be a safe place where he could disconnect and just enjoy himself. Second, as he thought about his next career move, he knew what he wanted to do even if he was not sure that it would work out.

* * *

As Sean was driving his navy blue, recent-model Audi through the streets of downtown Chicago to his breakfast meeting with Pat Scott, he contemplated how this week had just flown by. He and Pat were meeting at Lou Mitchell's, a famous Chicago restaurant known for its home-style breakfasts. Sean was surprised that Scott had gotten there early and already had a table. Sean chuckled as he arrived at the table and said, "It looks like you're finding your way around this city pretty well for a New Yorker."

Pat laughed and said, "If it was not for the cabbies, I would be lost."

After the coffee arrived, Sean asked, "How are things back at the System office?"

Pat replied, "The independent auditors are looking into the issue that took down Greene. In addition, I believe the Health System financials will get worse before they get better. I just hope the hospitals can produce more on their respective bottom lines over the next six months to help minimize the overall impact of some of the adjustments we will have to take at the Health System level." Sean just nodded and was thinking how there were some things about his old job he would never miss.

As breakfast was served, Sean took note of how healthy both Pat and he had ordered. Scott had ordered an egg-white omelet, fruit, and wheat toast, while Sean had ordered oatmeal with a large bowl of fresh fruit. Sean added, "Since I ran this morning, I want to keep up my healthy habits the rest of the day."

Scott said, "I do not know about you, but ten years ago, I was not eating this healthy. I had a cardiac health scare back when I was working on Long Island and that helped me to change my ways." Sean agreed and said it was when Kate finally got sober that he knew it was time for him to take control of his own health in order to live a longer life.

It seemed like no more than five seconds went by before Scott asked, "So where are you with the idea I mentioned on Monday?"

Sean thought, "Well, she can be direct when she wants to be." He then spoke, explaining, "I have been considering very carefully which direction I want to go with my next career opportunity. I loved being a CEO, and yet there are many things I no longer enjoy with that role. I have thought a great deal about the desperate need for a system-wide Succession and Leadership Plan, and I am really interested in this new opportunity for my career. That being said, I cannot in good conscience accept the position, as proposed, with me reporting to Steve Driver. I would rather turn down the opportunity than compromise my values. I really want to help you with developing the Succession and Leadership Development Plan but not at the cost of me reporting to someone I don't respect." Sean observed Scott's reaction as he was speaking, and he could tell that she was not pleased with what she had just heard.

Pat began by saying, "Sean, you have to decide if you still want to be the 'king' or the 'kingmaker.'"

Sean thought for a moment and said, "I do not have to be the 'king' any longer, and I am excited to be in the 'kingmaker' role to help you—but not while reporting to Driver. I don't want to be associated with that man or any of the remaining members of that Liars Club. They are bad news. To me this is a nonstarter."

Pat could tell that Sean was not going to move off of his position, but she also knew that she needed him in this new role. She spoke next. "Everyone I have spoken to from the Board to the Health System executive team members all say this is an HR initiative and that is where it should report."

Sean wasted no time in following up, "If that is your final decision, then I am not the person to lead this effort."

Pat grew frustrated and said, "Goddamn it, that was not the answer I was hoping for. We don't have time to go back and rethink this again."

Sean added, "I appreciate your concern and the situation you are in but I cannot in good conscience work for Driver."

Pat replied, "Okay, Sean, I am prepared to make your concession. So allow me to rephrase the offer: will you accept the position as the Senior Vice President of Succession and Leadership Development with it reporting directly to me?" Sean could see that her strong blue-collar upbringing was coming forth in this discussion. In the end, Pat was headstrong and not afraid of what others would say. Perhaps it was because her father was a retired New York Police officer and her two brothers were New York firefighters. Pat's only sister was an FBI agent assigned to high-profile cases out of the New York office. This heavy background of law enforcement highlighted the need to make quick decisions because when out in the field it could be the difference between life and death. Sean had also learned when researching Pat that she had received her MBA from the University of Pennsylvania Wharton School so he knew she was "no dummy."

Sean smiled and said, "If you are offering me the position as we discussed and with it reporting directly to you, then my answer is 'yes.' I will gladly accept your offer."

With that, Pat reached her hand across the table and said, "I am looking to forward to working with you."

Sean shook her hand and said, "I serve at the pleasure of the CEO."

8

THE HIGH COST OF TURNOVER

F OUR WEEKS LATER, Sean looked out at the Holy Spirit executive
team as he stood at the front of the boardroom and delivered the bad
news. "Ladies and gentlemen, our Health System is in serious trouble.
The hard truth is that we are just a few heart beats away from a major crisis."
Having Sister Elizabeth, the Board Chair, and some of the other Board members in the room hearing this bold statement made everyone except Pat and
Sean uncomfortable because the others had been telling the Board everything was "just fine."

It was time for Sean to present his findings of the past several weeks to
the Health System Board after he had personally conducted interviews of a total
of forty-eight leaders throughout the Health System office and the hospitals with
the goal of formulating an effective Succession and Leadership Development
Plan. The meeting was being held in the Health System boardroom, which was
referred to by everyone who worked in the hospitals as the "Gold Coast."

The hallways leading to the room were lined with mahogany panels and
the floors covered with handmade Burberry rugs. The boardroom itself was

outfitted with a thirty-foot, teak table and the latest electronic equipment—including video conferencing equipment that cost $150,000—and was rarely used. The executive assistants that worked on the Gold Coast joked that the astronauts in the orbiting space station could communicate with the Health System leadership if NASA ever lost its communication signal. As for the executive suites on the floor, each executive got to pick his or her own office furniture and there was an informal competition as to which office looked the best and cost the most.

Just being on this floor upset Sean because it was his and the other hospitals who had paid for these "extras" through the Health System assessments. Sean had to talk to himself privately so as not to get upset about the opulence of the offices and focus on the issue at hand, succession and leadership development planning.

During Miles Greene's tenure as CEO, there had been a clear division among the executive team when it came to appreciating Sean's contributions to the Health System. Some liked Sean and others did not; there was no middle ground. Those that liked him, and they were many, made him feel very welcome in the room today, while those with a strong dislike for him shook his hand while barely making eye contact. Sean knew the history of this part of the team was to try and "play nice" during the meeting and then "bitch and complain" about one another behind closed office doors or in the parking lot after the meeting ended.

Sean continued his announcement to the group. "As you know," Sean said, "our system is under investigation for falsifying quality data, and the System finances have taken a dramatic, negative turn. In fact, I believe our bonds may be downgraded once the 'Street' learns more about our systemic problems."

Father Jack Donnelly, Senior Vice President (SVP) of Mission for the Health System, dropped his pen upon hearing Sean's description of the financial woes facing his beloved Health System. As it turned out, Father Jack—a tall, athletic-looking Diocesan Priest, who also liked to cook and had a heavy

Irish accent—had never heard such statements come from Miles Greene in the past, since his style was to keep bad news confidential.

As Sean prepared to continue on, Tina Blake, the System CFO, leaned over and whispered to Steve Driver, "I got rid of Sean the last time; now it's your turn." In reality, it was both Tina Blake and Charles Brown who had "convinced" Miles Greene to force Sean's retirement, but Blake was not bashful about taking all of the credit.

"Believe it or not," Sean went on to the group, "those two concerns are just symptoms of a more serious problem. The real problem, I have learned after interviewing forty-eight different members of the Health System is that we do not now have the talent or the leadership depth to turn our situation around. Not now. Not in the future."

Father Jack, who had joked just before the meeting that everyone should get their soda bread orders in by noon as he'd be baking several batches this weekend, could not withhold his irritation any longer and asked directly to Steve Driver, "I thought you assured us just three months ago that we had all of the internal talent we would need for the next five to seven years!" Driver raised his eyebrows in disapproval but made no other effort to respond so Sean filled in the pregnant silence.

"The reality is that the healthcare industry is changing, and we do not have the business and leadership skill sets to be successful."

When Sean paused, Tina Blake stated quite loudly, "Sean, with all due respect, your characterization of the financial troubles is way overstated. We have been in tougher straits and made it through before, and we will do so again. I and my team just need a little more time to find some positive adjustments. And I might add if we had more support from the hospital CEOs, we would not be in this mess."

"Typical deflection on the part of Blake," Sean thought. "Always trying to blame someone else." There was a long silence with everyone wondering who was going to speak next, Sean or Tina.

Pat Scott surprised everyone when she jumped in and said, "Sean is right about our quality, financial, and leadership concerns. In fact, I believe we're going to be in really bad shape for the next two to three years. It will take us that long to fix our fundamental problems, especially as they relate to grooming and developing internal talent for the challenges ahead." There was a realization by everybody in the room that they had just experienced a sudden shift of power on the Health System executive team. No longer would Tina Blake be able to force her will on the entire group. Pat Scott had learned years ago that "there can only be one agenda and it is the agenda of the CEO." Today, she would have to assert that agenda.

Like Tina Blake, Steve Driver had wanted to push back on Sean. Instead, he quickly reconsidered after watching how Scott had just put Blake back in her place. Pat wondered whether Charles Brown might make a move next given her previous conversation with him. When Pat had called Brown to tell him about Sean rejoining the team, Brown had said with a raised voice, "As the acting Health System CEO, you got to do what you got to do. I don't care what you do with that SOB, Sean O'Brien, but keep him out of my hospital and tell him to stay away from Maryanne Richmond!"

For now, Brown remained silent.

Pat said, "Please continue, Sean."

Sean went on to share the results of his interviews, highlighting the gap between where things stood today and where the system needed to be in three to five years. It was huge.

In developing a customized Succession and Leadership Development Plan for the Health System, the questions Sean had asked were in three main categories:

1. What is the current status of the Health System?

2. Where does the Health System need to be in three to five years?

3. What business and leadership skills will be needed to achieve the three to five-years goals?

The first 2 questions dealt directly with the status of the organization, which was somewhat unusual for those who had been part of the previous Succession and Leadership Development planning at the Holy Spirit Health System, which had been conducted online. These questions were included because Sean had learned from his own career that you had to understand where the organization was and where it was going in order to determine what business and leadership skills would be needed to move the organization forward. It was a straightforward idea that was nonetheless often overlooked.

"As it turns out, our inpatient business model needs to transition to an outpatient-focused model that will then need to concentrate not only on outpatient testing volume but also on Population Health, which is focused on keeping patients healthy and out of the hospital. In the future, we will be paid mainly to keep people healthy." As a visual aid, Sean held up the cover of a news magazine on the topic, which had a picture of two running shoes and a glass of freshly squeezed orange juice.

"If we are going to be successful," Sean added, "we need to change our business model as well as our business and leadership skill sets."

Steve Driver raised his hand and asked with a bit of attitude, "To which model? To which skill sets?"

To introduce the needed skills, Sean explained the five-tool player term used in baseball. "A five-tool player is rare and is someone who can hit for average and power, who can field, who can throw, and who has speed. The same is true for a talented executive, who must have the basic hard skills: finance, quality, and strategy." Sean knew that it was the specifics of these three skills that would need to change at the Health System.

"Strategically," he said, "we need to explore and highlight how the services we offer are different from our closest competitor so we do not just appear as a mirror image of them. In addition, our financial skills need to be more focused on how we can negotiate agreements with payors and employers to keep individuals healthy and also be able to live within a set budgeted amount to take care of a group of employees. The days of being paid for every test and admission will soon be over. We will need actuarial and population management skills to be successful in this new era of healthcare. Quality outcomes will not only drive the business, but they will also relate to how we will be paid in the near future. And yes, we have become more focused on quality, but we will soon need to expand that to include a focus on extending our quality efforts into the home or workplace. Lastly, the 'new' soft skills will be focused in two main areas: emotional intelligence and communications skills." The mention of these last two skills seemed to raise some eyebrows so Sean continued, "A leader can be really strong in the basic strategy, finance, and quality skills, but if they are not able to get along and motivate others and effectively communicate, then they will be ineffective. This is one of the main reasons why individuals fail at the executive level."

Sean noticed Sister Elizabeth taking notes, which was her style given the twenty-three years she taught in high school. She raised her hand and asked, "I want to make sure I have those skills you just mentioned. You began with finance, strategy, and quality and then added communication and emotional Intelligence. Is that accurate?"

Sean paused to let Sister's question and response sink in with the others in the meeting, "Yes, Sister, that is exactly right."

The team was impressed by Sean's responses, which led Sister Elizabeth to say, "I see where you're going with this Sean, and I like it. But what confuses me is that you think we don't have the internal talent for it. In my view, there are a number of individuals in the system who have a lot of potential to lead us."

Sean thought for a second and answered, "Fair enough. I might think the same if I hadn't just conducted almost fifty interviews that revealed otherwise. The results seem to show that we just don't have the internal talent to fill many of the anticipated vacancies. For example, there is no one in the organization who has population management skills, and also most of our leaders will need to develop new negotiation skills to be successful in the world of healthcare reform."

"So how are we going to develop sufficient leaders for tomorrow?" Sister Elizabeth asked.

Sean smiled and continued, "First, we need to identify at least twelve individuals within the Health System that we believe could become strong leaders over the next two years. Next, we need to dedicate time, money, and educational resources to further developing the business and leadership skills that will be needed to prepare these leaders for the challenges ahead. It's not a matter of just hiring and promoting," he said.

Sean went on to explain that approximately 40% of executives that start in a new position fail within the first 18 months on the job. Sean added, "We need to support these new leaders in order to improve their chances of success because a recruitment failure can be incredibly costly."

Father Jack spoke, saying, "Sean, as you know, I am not a finance person. What do you mean, it's costly?"

Sean got up and walked over to the easel that he was going to use to illustrate his point. He began by asking a question of Steve Driver. "Steve, what is the average salary for a hospital CEO within our Health System?"

Driver was somewhat surprised that Sean had called on him and finally collected his thoughts and answered, "Let's say the average is $400,000."

Sean then wrote that figure down in green marker on the big piece of paper and then asked, "If a hospital CEO needed to be replaced, how much would it cost?" Others around the table chimed in that it could cost between six to eight times the CEO's salary between severance, recruitment, and "lost opportunity costs." Sean wrote "6 to 8 times salary" on the top right-hand corner of the paper and then said, "Let's be conservative and say it will cost four times the CEO's salary." So below the $400,000 salary number, he wrote "× 4 = $1,600,000" to highlight the cost to replace a CEO.

Some people around the table were not surprised by this figure while others looked shocked. Reilly Fitzmaurice, SVP for Strategic Planning and a redhead with a fiery temper to match, raised her hand and asked, "Are you telling me every time we have to replace a CEO with someone from the outside it can cost the Health System $1.6 million dollars?"

Sean used the delayed response to let the magnitude of the question sink in and then added, "Yes, Reilly, that is exactly what I'm saying." Reilly could not contain her shock at that figure of $1.6 million dollars.

Sean continued, "But that is not the total cost of an unsuccessful CEO recruitment. Research has highlighted that once a new CEO is on board, up to *one half* of the executive team will leave or be replaced within eighteen months." This last tidbit caught almost everyone in the room by surprise because they had never thought that far through the impact of a CEO departure. It also hit home with everyone in the room that up to one half of the individuals sitting around this big, expensive boardroom table might be gone once the new Health System CEO was in place.

Sean sensed this change and proceeded to ask Driver, "What is the average salary for a hospital-level, senior team member?"

Driver responded, "The average is $250,000." Sean drew a line below the $1,600,000 figure and added "$250,000 × 4 times salary = $1,000,000." The four times represented the same "cost" associated with a departing VP as with a departing CEO.

Next Sean asked those around the table, "How many leaders are on the average hospital executive team?" There was some back and forth, and finally the group reached agreement that the number was probably something close to eight.

Sean then wrote the number "4" below the "$1,000,000" figure and said, "So if four members of an executive team leave within eighteen months, then the additional cost to the hospital is $4,000,000. And remember we must also add back the cost of the CEO turnover, which was on average $1,600,000, so the total cost of a hospital for losing a CEO is approximately $5,600,000. This is the hidden cost of executive turnover that we fail to see yet feel the effects of every time a hospital CEO departs and we need to fill from the outside." Sean put the cap on the marker and turned to face the table. "Any questions?" he asked. Nothing. The room had gone completely silent.

Pat Scott spoke next and asked Sean, "How many CEO/Executives are expected to retire in the next three to five years within the Health System?"

Sean knew this answer but let some time pass before saying, "There are at least six hospital CEOs that will retire over the next three to six years, plus some of the individuals sitting around this table." At this point, both Father Jack and Reilly Fitzmaurice were looking for their calculators to do the math on what Sean had just shared.

"All in all, I believe there will be at least eight senior executives of the Holy Spirit Health System who will retire or depart over the next three to five years. So if we multiply the total cost of a departing CEO, which we just illustrated, it will cost our system approximately $5,600,000 × 8 departing executives or a total of $44,800,000. As a result, a Health System that is already struggling financially will be faced with almost $45 million dollars of costs related to executive turnover in just the next three to five years. That, my friends, is a cost we cannot afford to bear." It was an amount higher than anyone in the room had ever anticipated.

Silence hung over the room like cigarette smoke over an old sporting event in an indoor area. "As you can imagine," Pat Scott said, breaking the silence, "Sean has been hard at work creating a proposed Succession and Leadership Development Plan for the Health System to help address this challenge. We want the rest of your buy-in to make it work. Sean, can you review the plan?"

Sean proceeded to propose that twelve high-potential leaders be recruited into a team with the sole purpose of developing them as the "farm system" for when future positions became available within the Health System. Sean handed out the list of names as well as an analysis of the costs associated with educating each of the twelve high-potential leaders.

First, someone asked why there wasn't at least one representative from each of the hospitals. Sean's response was, "Unfortunately, some of our teams are so weak they didn't warrant having someone be part of this new team."

Next, Reilly Fitzmaurice, who was becoming more animated the more she learned about this topic, asked why there were twelve members when only eight slots would need to be filled. Reilly's interest in this topic aligned with her responsibility for producing the strategic plan for the Health System, and she realized that with each CEO turnover the chances for "her" plan being successfully implemented decreased dramatically.

Sean responded, "The reality is that some of the twelve will not make it through the process due to a variety of reasons. Some will not want to do the work that is required; others will not be able to make the commitment in time and effort to successfully complete the program." Sean added that the cost to develop each individual who would be part of the Succession Planning effort would be $200,000 per member.

Realizing that he had just provided a great deal of information to the group, Sean decided to stop and allow everyone time to review the list of high-potential individuals and digest all they had just learned.

Reilly asked, "There are some very talented leaders whose names are not on this list. Why?"

Sean responded, "There is a big difference between someone who is a high performer and someone with high potential. A main difference between a high performer and someone who has high potential is that the high potential has ability but also has aspiration and engagement qualities to succeed at the next level. He or she has the desire to get to the next level and willingness to actually do the work. In contrast, if someone with great talent does not have the ambition to get to the next level nor the desire to do the work, their chances of success are slim. Research highlights that only 29% of high performers actually are successful at the next level. The best way to answer this is to think about someone whom you know who is a really good nurse that got promoted and then failed at the next level. That person was very good at a floor nurse level, but that success did not transfer to the management level. We often assume because the person had success at one level that success will follow them wherever they go, but that simply is not true."

Steve Driver added, "That is exactly what happened with a very talented ICU nurse of ours who we talked into taking a nursing management job. In spite of our best efforts to support her, she left the hospital after being in the new job only fourteen months. She hated her new job, and because she felt like a failure, she left us without ever giving us a chance to find her another position within the Health System."

It was Father Jack who tried to summarize, "So if we do nothing, our system could take a $44,800,000 blow if this entire turnover hits as expected. But if we invest in the development of our leaders at the cost of $200,000 × 12 = $2,400,000, we could be saving the approximately $42.4 million in recruitment and lost opportunity costs?"

Sean replied with excitement, "Yes! And that is why we need to begin this program *as soon as possible.*"

Father Jack responded, "I would say that is a good return on our investment."

The last question was from Sister Elizabeth, who asked, "What is wrong with recruiting a new CEO or other leaders from outside the organization?"

Sean answered, "Pat and I spoke about this very question when we first met, and in short there is nothing wrong with recruiting someone from the outside but only under these four conditions: need for a financial turnaround, need to reestablish credibility, need for a new strategic direction, or need for a culture change. Outside of those four reasons, every effort should be made to develop internal talent. Internal talent already knows the culture, history, and how things 'get done' within the organization. An outsider has to learn all of these things, which takes a lot of time and effort. Developing internal talent will enhance the effectiveness of the new leader starting from the first day on the job."

Sister Elizabeth just smiled at Sean's answer and said "thank you" because her point was made as to how she was in support of developing internal talent to address the leadership needs of the Health System. The last example seemed to work for the entire team as well, and Sean wrapped his presentation up in less time than was given on the agenda. Sean asked if there were any other questions, and upon hearing none, he thanked the group for their attention and began to pack up to leave the meeting.

Sean felt relieved as he walked out of the boardroom, glad that he had put his best effort forward and sensing that he had gotten through to the group. Pat Scott briefly joined him in the hall to thank him for his work and to congratulate him on his strong delivery of the topic and their respective game plan. Sean could feel the tightness in his lower back begin to loosen as he headed to the elevator and then gave Pat a quick wave goodbye. He wondered what, if any, changes the executive team would make to the list of twelve names he had proposed.

* * *

Sean's cell phone rang just as he was arriving back at his office at the Wellness Center. It was Pat, who said, "Good job, Sean. The executive team was totally in support of the commencement of this initiative as well as of you being responsible for implementing the plan." This was a far cry from just a few months ago when Sean had been forced out of the organization.

Pat cleared her throat and added the following: "You should know, however, that there was a request to add one more person to the Succession Plan team."

Sean asked with a slight edge in his voice, "Let me guess who the request came from? Was it one Tina Blake or Steve Driver?"

Pat responded quite quickly, "Yes. Tina wants Maria Smith, the controller of the Health System, added to the Succession Planning team. Given the way I pinned Tina's ears back during the beginning stages of your presentation, I decided to honor this request."

Sean thought for moment and then added, "I'm okay with adding Maria to the group as long as Tina is aware that adding a thirteenth individual to this process increases the cost of the program by $200,000." What he wanted to say in protest was how Maria Smith did not fit the true definition of a high potential but was more like a high performer who had a high chance of failing at the next level. But again he thought it better to leave some things unsaid.

"Isn't it interesting," he thought, "how adding Maria Smith will make for lucky number thirteen of the Succession Planning group."

9

THE CURSE OF THE GIFT

THAT NIGHT, SEAN treated himself to a steak dinner and a glass of red wine at his favorite restaurant, Charlie Trotter's, while replaying the meeting with the Health System executive team in his mind. As he took a bite of his baked potato, he couldn't help but stop and grin, realizing that his meeting was a success and the new Succession and Leadership Development program was about to be launched.

Yes, the addition of Maria to the group was troubling, but he finally decided he could not worry about one person when the other twelve and the entire Health System could benefit from this program. Sean's last statement to Pat Scott was that he was okay with the addition of Maria Smith but he wanted to meet with her separately before the first meeting of the Succession Planning group. At this meeting, he wanted to "calibrate the expectations" for Maria and her interactions with the rest of the team. Pat agreed and told Sean that she would have Maria call him first thing tomorrow morning to set up some time to meet.

The next morning, Maria called Tina Blake to tell her she was not going to go to the meeting with Sean.

"Listen," Tina said, "I had to fight to get you into that program. Now I need you to go and attend all of the meetings so I know what is going on."

Maria called Tina out on this statement, saying, "What do you mean you had to fight to get me into this group? I am one of the top financial performers throughout the system, and according to many others I am one of the top up-and-coming executives in the System."

Tina paused for quite a bit because she now realized she had not paid attention to when Sean was explaining in Monday's meeting just how the original twelve team members were identified. She finally said, "That's a great question to ask O'Brien when you meet with him tomorrow morning."

Maria was not satisfied with that answer but made a mental note to ask Sean that very question. She was now fired up and when she was in this type of mood, she could become downright nasty to others. Maria said in anger, "This is bull!"

"Listen, Maria, my hope is that O'Brien will screw up again and we can get rid of him once and for all. Nothing good is going to come out of this development effort, but I want to make sure I know what is going on so I know when to pull the plug on this 'special project.'"

Maria knew enough about negotiation that she needed to stop her resistance before she might alienate Tina, who had been her advocate and protector for many years. Maria finally said, "Alright, I will be the good soldier and become part of the program. But I want it noted that I am not happy with how this whole thing went down."

It was 8:15 AM on Wednesday when Maria walked in to Sean's office, with an air of annoyance trailing behind her. Before Sean could say, "welcome" or "please have a seat," Maria asked quite rudely, "Why was I not picked to be part of this group from the outset, and why did Blake have to fight to get me on it?"

Sean paused because his initial reaction was to meet Maria's tone with an equally angry response because he was not going to let her get the upper hand in this discussion. Instead, he controlled himself and responded, "Good morning. I'm glad you could make it to discuss your potential role in joining the Succession and Leadership Development team."

Sean's response made Maria even angrier. She fumed, "What do you mean *potential* role with this group? I'm already part of it according to Tina Blake, and you have no say as to whether I stay or go."

Sean was trying to keep an open mind about Maria, however, she was doing nothing to help her case. Sean countered with, "Pat Scott has given me full authority over this effort, from the recruitment on through to the content we will cover. To be honest, I did not pick you to be part of this program. In fact, I believe your chances of success are quite small. Yes, you are a 'high performer.' Yes, you have top-of-the-industry financial skills. But you severely lack interpersonal and communication skills from everything I've seen and heard. The reason you are here is because Pat Scott supported Tina's request to have you added to the group. So let me be perfectly clear, if I believe you or any other member of the team will be problematic or is not making a sincere effort to improve, then I can make whatever changes are needed to ensure the success of this effort."

Maria opened her mouth to say something and then heard Blake's voice in her head stopping her. Instead of speaking, she grabbed a ponytail holder from her pocket and pulled her thick black hair into a tight bun so she could think more clearly.

Over the seven years Maria had worked at the Holy Spirit Health System, Sean had learned a great deal about her and her healthcare career. After graduating from Long Island University with a degree in accounting, Maria went to work with one of the "Big Four" accounting firms. For the first 3 years, she moved between different departments, which was normal for a new grad right out of college. The hours were long, travel was brutal, and the work demanding, but Maria didn't seem to mind. Eventually, she caught the eye of one of the healthcare partners, Kevin Parker, who recruited her to join his team. Kevin noticed Maria had a very assertive, bordering on aggressive, personality when dealing with coworkers and sometimes clients, but he hoped with time and some mentoring this would become less of an issue. Kevin had a good reputation for developing talent so Maria jumped at the opportunity.

Over the next five years, Maria's skills grew. She went from working on small hospital audits to working on large health system audits. When the Holy Spirit Health System wanted a "new set of eyes" on their audit, Kevin Parker assigned the account to Maria on a one-year "trial basis." Almost immediately, Maria and Tina Blake hit it off. Maria felt she could learn a great deal working alongside of Blake, who was quite a success within the ranks of CFOs throughout the country. She had become the Holy Spirit CFO at the age of 43 and continued to enjoy success at the Health System. Maria also liked Tina's "don't take any crap from anybody, especially men" attitude and felt their personalities would work well together. Maria even commented to a coworker back at the accounting firm that "working with Tina Blake will also get me away from Parker and his weak efforts to try and change my personality."

In turn, Tina was pleased with the work Maria had completed during the first year of the assignment and requested that she be assigned to the account full time. Not wanting to lose the Health System business, the firm assigned Maria permanently to the account, even though Kevin Parker expressed some reservations that Tina Blake may not be the best "role model" for Maria at this stage of her career. The other partners were more concerned about keeping the account than about Maria's career development, which was not the first time this situation had happened amongst the firm's partners.

Maria's status with Tina Blake took a major positive turn during her second year working on the Health System account. Maria had discovered major problems with how the Health System was calculating the amount of bad debt to be written off. The error meant the Health System had undervalued the amount that they should have been writing off to bad debt for the past five years. In order to correct his problem, the Health System would have to make a "major write off" in the amount of $19 million in the current fiscal year. When Maria shared this problem with Tina in her office, Tina could tell that Maria was quite nervous and concerned about the severity of the problem. Upon hearing the news, Tina immediately thought about how this not only would be a major hit to the finances of the Health System but also to her career.

Tina said, "Let's not tell anybody about this for obvious reasons and give me a few days to see if I can find some reserves to cover this problem."

Maria knew she should be telling Kevin Parker about this issue but also wanted to impress Tina Blake. Maria also knew there were no reserves on the books that could possibly cover this major of a hit since she had just completed the review of all areas where reserves could be "hidden." Still, Maria agreed to keep the issue quiet, and sure enough within three days Tina told her that the State of Illinois would be granting the Health System a "one-time" payment of $22 million to cover an unusually high amount of free care provided to the residents of the State. The extra State money effectively covered the problem, and, soon after, Maria became the Controller for the Holy Spirit Health System, leaving Kevin Parker and the accounting firm behind. Only a few knew—including Greene, Driver, and Brown—that Tina had rewarded Maria for being a "team player" with this newly created position. Funny how certain things work out for some when deals are made behind closed doors.

Sean knew all about Maria's tight relationship with Tina Blake, but he was damn sure he was not going to allow Maria or Tina to mess up his Succession and Leadership Development Team. Still, Sean suddenly remembered something that Maryanne had said to Sean just before his meeting with Maria this morning when she called to say, "Just give Maria a chance. If anyone can help her, it is you."

Sean took a deep breath and decided to give Maria the benefit of the doubt. He truly hoped that things would work out and she would become part of the program and benefit from the efforts. Sean also thought about how he must come up with a name for this group since calling it the Succession and Leadership Development Team was too damn long.

Sean said, "Let me address your original question about how we selected members of this team. You are right, Maria, that you are what we consider a high performer within the Health System, meaning you produce strong results compared to your annual goals and objectives. This is supported by your above-average performance evaluations and merit increases and incentive payouts. But research has shown that only 29% of high performers actually perform well at the next level." Maria felt surprised by Sean's bluntness, and yet in a strange way she welcomed it.

Sean continued, "When I presented for the Health System's executive team on Monday, I used the example of how we often will take a clinically strong nurse and promote her into a management role. We assume just because he or she excelled at the 'bedside' that they will also excel with managing people, overseeing budgets, and producing strong quality outcomes. Some make the transition, while many others do not and often feel like they failed. In fact, I believe it is the organization who failed the individual by taking him or her out of their element and moving them into management. This means achieving results is not the only barometer for predicting success when considering someone for a promotion."

"Individuals who succeed at the next level not only have to be strong in the hard skills like finance, strategy, and quality, they also have to be strong in the soft skills like emotional intelligence and communication skills. Those five skills—strategy, quality, finance, emotional intelligence, and communication skills—plus determining a leader's ability to aspire and engage at the next level are what I considered when developing the list of twelve to form this first group. In all honesty, Maria, you are really strong in the three hard skills—finance, strategy, and quality—but you are weak in the two soft skills, emotional intelligence and communication. I also believe you do not aspire to be successful at the next level and that you are not willing to put in the work needed to move forward. You have what I call the 'curse of the gift.'"

"What the hell does 'curse of the gift' mean?" said Maria, who appeared physically upset by this last comment.

"The curse of the gift means you are blessed with some really great skills but they become a hindrance because they make you feel like you do not have to develop any more. You are like an all-star athlete who feels he or she does not have to practice to get better. The reality of this work is it is oftentimes easier to develop the hard skills and often very challenging to develop the soft skills. I initially did not feel you would be willing to hear this candid feedback, put in the work, and be willing to change in order to be considered as part of this team."

Sean paused and waited for Maria to respond, but he could tell that she had been rocked by what she just heard him say about her strengths and weakness. He was not quite sure how to read this uncomfortable interaction because it was so unlike Maria to be silent.

Maria finally spoke and said, "Sean, my ultimate step in my career plan is to become a health system CFO someday, and I believe the next logical step would be for me to become a hospital CFO. I have had a career plan for years and so far it has worked out well for me. In order for me to become a hospital and health system CFO, you might be right though. It's possible that I am going to have to develop other skills in order to be successful. I'm not sure if that's true, but I'm willing to consider it if it will help me reach my goals."

Now it was Sean who was stunned at what he just heard from Maria because he now knew Maria did aspire to be successful at the next level and apparently she was willing to engage with others to attain her career goals. Sean finally spoke and said, "I will be honest Maria, prior to this meeting, I was looking for a reason to keep you out of this program, but after what you just shared, I am willing to give you a chance. If you can see the need for growth, then there is some hope. But if you do not do the work or become disruptive to the rest of the team, I will bounce you off this team so fast your head will spin. Am I making myself clear?"

Maria said yes, though Sean could not tell if she really meant it. What Maria was really thinking about was what Sean had just said, and she was remembering some of the same feedback she had received from Kevin Parker, her boss back at the accounting firm. Maria was beginning to think, "Maybe there is some truth to these concerns expressed by Kevin and Sean, and it might be time to do something about it." She even thought about Sean's comment about improving her communication skills. "I could have expressed my interest in this team with more energy and affirmation," she admitted. As Maria got up to leave and shook Sean's hand, they both agreed to see each other at the program kick-off meeting next Thursday.

After the meeting ended, Sean sat in his office, writing up notes from the conversation he had just had with Maria. He chuckled, thinking, "Here I was looking for a reason to bounce her out of this program, and at the end I allow her to stay. Who knew she had a career plan and that it involved the next two career moves? Shoot, maybe I will ask her to help teach the career plan lesson to the rest of the team."

Admittedly, Sean was still having some doubts about how a "tiger could change its stripes," but a little voice in his head was telling him to give Maria a chance. He was thinking that he must be feeling the influence of not just Maryanne but also his wife Kate, who was always pulling for the "underdog." Before putting the Maria Smith file away, he thought, "I hope I'm not making a big mistake. One bad actor in a program like this could ruin everything."

10

INDIVIDUAL TALENTS
VS. TEAM TALENTS

ARRANGEMENTS WERE MADE for the Succession and Leadership Development group to meet at the new Admiral on the Lake. This was a brand new, assisted-living facility located on the North Shore of the Lake. The Admiral was founded in 1858 as the oldest nonprofit organization dedicated to creating senior living to address the needs of Chicago-area seniors. Upon their entering the conference room, many of the members of the Succession and Leadership Development group seemed confused. The room was not set up in a traditional meeting configuration but instead had seven large "bingo" type tables with a white table cloth covering something big on the top of each table. Sean asked everyone to meet around him, and he proceeded to congratulate them for being selected to be part of the Succession and Leadership Development Program. Sean added, "And don't worry, before we leave this week, we will come up with a better name for our group."

This comment generated some nervous laughter from the group, which did seem to relieve some of the stress in the room. Before today, Sean had spoken to everyone individually about the expectations of this program and had explained why and how they were selected to be part of this group. Most of the participants felt honored or excited to have been chosen, many felt nervous, and others wondered if this program would deliver on its promise to prepare them for the next level of leadership. Maria felt skeptical.

"Since we do not know one another," Sean said, "I have devised a 'get to know you' activity. Behind me, you will find several tables. I'd like you to break up into six groups of two—one group at each table." Individuals began to walk toward the tables hesitantly because they did not know what was going to come next; some of them resented having to find a partner.

Sister Jeannie Grant, VP for Mission & Ministry from St. Mary's Hospital, was left standing at a table all by herself. Sister Jeannie was rather tall at six feet even and looked almost malnourished due mainly from her years of mission work in Peru. Sean walked over to Sister Jeannie and said, "I will be your partner." Sean had temporarily forgotten to consider that the group was made up of thirteen and would not divide evenly.

Sister Jeannie had never been one to hide her emotions, which were always on display on her face. Upon realizing who her partner would be, she looked somewhat shocked and mad to be working with Sean. Sean could not tell which emotion was stronger, but it did not really matter since both were negative.

Sean and Sister Jeannie knew each other from over the years, and Sister Jeannie was not a big fan of his. Sean could never figure out what he had done to cause the friction, but he knew it had existed for at least ten years. Sean remembered thinking, "My guess is that she's Irish because they have been known to carry grudges for centuries." He hoped that the following exercise would produce an opportunity for him to learn why she did not seem to like him.

Now that everyone had a partner, Sean asked someone at each table to remove the table cloth that was covering the large object. As the cloths were removed, everyone could see that the large object underneath was a box that contained either a pink or blue tricycle. Still, looks of bewilderment prevailed on everyone's face.

"Now I know you are all probably wondering why there is a box containing a children's tricycle on each table. Well, my friends, we are going to build the tricycles together today and throughout the process hopefully get to know one another. The only instructions I will provide is that the tricycle must be assembled properly, and the first group to complete the task will get a prize."

With that, everyone began trying to assemble the bikes. Soon, many learned that the assignment was harder than imagined. As Sister Jeannie began to unpack the box and Sean circulated around the room, he noticed how some other teams were tearing into the box, removing pieces and not even paying attention to the instructions. In fact, Maria Smith and Donna Reuss at Table 1 appeared to be most focused on getting the bike built first and "winning." This surprised Sean somewhat since he expected this from Maria but not Donna.

Donna was the COO of St. Luke's Hospital and someone who had come up through the ranks, starting in healthcare as a social worker. Donna had been the COO at St. Luke's hospital for the past four years; her next career step would be to become a CEO of one of the Hospitals within the Health System. Perhaps Donna's approach to the tricycle was best captured when she, the mother of two children, was overheard saying, "My husband Gerry and I have put many of these together on Christmas Eve so we won't even need the instructions."

At Table 2 was Cheryl Butler, COO from St. Francis Hospital, and Jim Piper, the CHRO from Nativity Hospital. Cheryl had come up through the ranks of the hospital, starting as a nurse, next becoming a nurse manager, and then holding the role as Chief Nursing Officer at St. Francis Hospital. Jim Piper was a natural HR Leader and not only had a great way with people but also had a God-given gift of being able to hire well qualified and talented leaders. Sean thought that if Jim could educate the others on how to interview and hire great talent, it would be a great gift to everyone. Unlike Maria and Donna, both Cheryl and Jim were meticulous about following the directions. The saying "slow but steady wins the race" came to mind when Sean considered how they were approaching the task at hand.

Blake Jones, the CEO of St. James Community Hospital, stood at Table 3 and welcomed the opportunity to work with Harry Klein, VP of Operations at one of the System's hospitals. Since Blake and Harry were both from small "rural access" hospitals, they had been on numerous committees together and had even gone ice fishing together. Since being the CEO for two years of a twenty-five-bed hospital, Blake was used to "wearing many hats"; his goal was to become a CEO of a larger, more complicated hospital. Harry was the VP of Operations at Immaculate Conception Hospital, one of the smallest hospitals within the system with only eighteen inpatient beds and no OB unit. Sean could never understand how a hospital with the name Immaculate Conception could not have an OB unit and apparently never had one.

During Sean's interviews, Harry had expressed an interest in becoming either a CEO of a small rural access hospital or a COO of a larger hospital within the system. Harry's hospital had been losing money for the past two years but to no fault of Harry. He was trying everything possible to turn that place around, which is what caught Sean's attention to make him part of this group. Sean was concerned that if Harry did not get some other experiences soon, his career could be tarnished if Immaculate Conception Hospital were to close.

At one point, it seemed like Blake and Harry were having too much fun. Sean called out, "Hope you guys are having some success with the assignment!" to which Blake responded, "Once you've spent time ice fishing with someone, you get to know one another real well and you learn to laugh a lot."

They seemed to be doing just fine, though both seemed a bit uncoordinated when it came to using the tools needed to build the tricycle.

Right next to Harry and Blake were Kylene Knight and Rachel Pepper, MD. Kylene was the CNO at Divine Mercy Hospital and someone Sean knew well from their having worked together. Kylene was a former military nurse and rose through the ranks of leadership with ease. Most of that success was due to her military training and also her strong interpersonal skills. Kylene just seemed to "get" people and was well respected by both nurses and physicians. Rachel Pepper, MD, was trained as an orthopedic surgeon at the Duke University and in her spare time also received her MBA from Duke's Fuqua School of Business. Rachel was an extremely bright and talented surgeon who specialized in treating and returning high-end athletes to active competition.

Sean thought that the pairing of Kylene and Rachel could not have worked out any better since Rachel was known for being too abrupt and short with people in general, but especially with nurses. Rachel was one of the last members to make the group because of her "challenging" interpersonal skills, but Sean knew that if she became stronger in this one area, she could become an excellent hospital CEO. Kylene, sensing Rachel's strong personality asked, "So where would you like to begin?" Given such an open invitation, Rachel went into full authoritative mode and started barking orders. Sean wondered if he was going to need a referee whistle to separate these two highly successful women.

The next table, Table 5, consisted of two of the most talented individuals within the system: Mike Polaski, COO at St. Roberta Hospital, and Tom Flowers, DO/CMO, from St. Agnes Medical Center. Mike Polaski was a very talented executive and someone who had a reputation for getting things done. In addition, Mike's reputation in the community was enhanced as he became a strong advocate for children born with Autism. Mike's younger daughter, Emma, was born with Autism, and Mike and his family had worked really hard to make sure Emma was well-integrated into the everyday life of their household and community. Tom Flowers, DO, was a Family Physician and a strong family man, known throughout the community for going into the emergency room at any time of day or night to help a friend or family member. Tom was new to the administrative side of healthcare but someone who was not afraid of taking on a new challenge.

The last table that seemed to be taking the early lead in the assignment of putting the tricycle together had Simon Gratz, the Chief Marketing Officer for Trinity Hospital and Jane Bing, VP for the Cardiac Service Line at Nazareth Hospital.

Since Sean was giving out the instructions and making sure everyone was at least getting started on their assignment, he was late returning to his table with Sister Jeannie. Sean was surprised to see that Sister Jeannie did not wait for him to return to begin the assignment. In fact, Sister Jeannie had things well under control with all parts organized in neat piles and the instructions being followed every step of the way.

During the pre-selection interviews with Sister Jeannie, she had expressed concern that in the past, members of her religious community had become CEOs just because they were nuns. Sister Jeannie wanted to become a hospital CEO someday, but she wanted to earn that right with having the proper education and experience. Sister Jeannie had graduated with an MBA in Health Administration from the Loyola University. For the past three years, she had been working as the VP of Mission at St. Mary's Hospital and was also very active with many operational and financial committees throughout the Health System.

"So how can I help, Sister Jeannie?" Sean asked, reengaging his partner. Sister Jeannie was not sure if Sean was referring to the assignment of assembling the bike or with something broader like her career.

"I have fourteen nieces and nephews and have helped put many a bicycle and tricycle together in my day," Sister Jeannie said. "So I think we are good.

Even though we might not be the first to complete the assignment, I will guarantee you our bike will be assembled properly and will make any child smile."

Sean thought to himself how self-assured and confident Sister Jeannie sounded and how that was a key factor in the success of any executive. Sister Jeannie continued, "But if you would like to help me with my career, you can begin by explaining why you ignored my requests to become part of your Board for the past several years." This caught Sean by total surprise because he wondered how Sister knew of his efforts to block her requests to become a part of his Board. He thought quickly and decided to follow his wife's advice when giving feedback to be "kind and direct."

Sean began, "Sister, I must admit to you that I did not want you on our Board, but it is probably not for the reasons you may believe. I imagine that you thought I did not want you on the Board because of your commitment to the poor and underserved in the community. The real reason was that I just felt you were too idealistic and needed more time to understand the workings of the hospital before you could balance your ardent activism with making the hard business decisions necessary to run a financially viable hospital. I believed that you needed more time to further develop before we offered you a position on the Board." Just after Sean finished what he was saying, he knew that Sister Jeannie's response could go really bad or really well. He hoped it would go well since a blow-up between he and the Sister could negatively impact the rest of the group.

After what seemed like a really long pause, Sister Jeannie responded, "Sean you are not the first one to hint that my aggressive stance on issues can be a problem, but you are the first one to really spell it out so clearly. I guess my aggressive nature is due to my many years as a missionary in Peru."

Sean added, "I believe being candid is the best way for leaders to communicate. I also appreciate your willingness to hear this difficult message."

"What I just heard from you was hard to hear but something I probably need to change in order to grow as both a professional and as a person. Will you help me to become a really strong healthcare executive that can make the hard business decisions and also remain true to my personal and religious values?"

Sean smiled and said, "I welcome the opportunity to work closely with you. I would like nothing more than to help you achieve your goals." It was as if the tension between them dissolved right at that moment and they seemed to form the kind of new, strong connection that often occurs when people are honest in dealing with a difficult situation.

Just then, Maria and Donna yelled out simultaneously, "Hold it everyone. We're done! We won!" As they lifted up the tricycle to show everyone their accomplishment, one of the back wheels fell off the bike, sending the wheel, washer, bolts, and nuts flying across the floor. Maria became so upset that she could not even help find the missing parts; her delay knocked them out of the competition altogether.

The winners instead were Kylene Knight and Rachel Pepper, MD, who finished about four minutes after the failed attempt of Maria and Donna. Sean watched with interest as both Kylene and Rachel seemed to compliment each other on the great job they did in assembling the tricycle. Knowing the challenges that Rachel had had with nurses, Sean wondered what it was about working with Kylene that enabled Rachel to appear to be such a team member. Maybe more good was coming out of this exercise than Sean had even intended.

After Sean gave Kylene and Rachel each their prize (a $100 gift certificate to Curtis Duffy's restaurant), Sean asked everyone to finish building the trikes. Within ten minutes, all teams were done and satisfied with their efforts. Sean then asked the group, "So what did you learn from this exercise?"

Donna Reuss responded first: "Putting a bike together is so much like life. Both are so much easier if you follow the instructions." That got a laugh out of everyone in the room, even Maria Smith, her partner.

Next, Mike Polaski said, "I thought the exercise was hard at the beginning because I felt Tom and I were both trying to do our own thing. This only made things much harder. Once we began to work together and use Tom's talents to understand the instructions and my talents to use the tools, we started to see real progress." It seemed like the other members of the group agreed with this assessment, nodding while realizing how it still took some teams longer than others to finish the task at hand.

After the laughter and conversation died down, Sean began, "There are two lessons to be learned from this exercise. First, like Donna said earlier, putting the tricycle together was much easier if you followed the instructions provided. I believe the same can be said about life in that if we have the benefit of strong mentors we can tap into their wisdom and we will get farther more quickly. Being a 'free agent' and going off and doing your own thing in large organizations will not be enough to get it done. There are many great frameworks we will learn together to help you all become strong, effective leaders within our Health System."

"Second, like Mike pointed out, the ability to work as part of a team is the fundamental ingredient for success. Using our individual talents for the greater good is what separates a mediocre team from a high performing team. We as executives will be known for the results we produce and we cannot produce anything while working alone."

This message seemed to really resonate well with the group. Sean then asked for other thoughts and observations about the tricycle exercise. Finally, Sister Jeannie said, "I learned a great deal from the exercise, but I also learned a lot about my teammate, Sean. I am sure I can learn a great deal more working with each one of you, and I welcome any and all feedback, both positive and constructive. It will be your feedback that will help me reach my goal to one day become a hospital CEO."

Others were nodding their heads in agreement, and finally Tom Flowers, DO, spoke up: "What are we going to do with these beautiful bikes?" Sean could not have asked for a better setup so he proceeded to make a quick phone call. One minute later, Sean's former executive assistant, Erin Carey, appeared with seven little children from the local day care agency that specialized in providing services for underprivileged children.

After the children were all assembled in a straight line in front of the room, Sean stood and said, "The last part of this assignment is for us to find joy in our work. We thought this would be a wonderful opportunity to donate these seven tricycles to these beautiful youngsters." With that, each team member got up and handed the freshly assembled tricycle to one of the seven children. Each child was so polite in saying, "thank you," and Sean even saw a few tears in the eyes of some of the members of the group.

* * *

"It is the dream of Pat Scott, our new system CEO, to develop the leadership and business skills of the next generation of leaders for our Health System," Sean explained, after the group reconvened at 10:15 AM and he had begun to share the goals and expectations for the program.

Cheryl Butler hesitantly raised her hand and asked, "Why has this become such a priority?"

Sean took the team through the same cost calculation that he did with the Health System executive team, basically highlighting that every time a hospital CEO departed, it cost the hospital $5.6 million. That cost included the cost of the departing CEO of approximately $1.6 million plus the cost to replace the half of the executive team that would leave approximately eighteen months after the next CEO was hired, estimated at $4 million.

There was a collective blank look on the faces of everyone in the room, and finally Mike Polaski said, "Wow, I never knew that the cost associated with a CEO leaving was so high. When I think about when our previous CEO left several years ago, I remember now that about one half of our executive team really did leave within the next year and a half. So I guess what I am saying is that even though those numbers are extremely high, I see now that they are very real. I am starting to really get the true cost impact of CEO turnover."

Sean went on to add, "The true impact is not just on the cost of the turnover but on the overall culture of the organization," Sean said. "There is research out there highlighting that up to 70% of an organization's culture is directly related to the CEO. So every time there is a CEO departure, the culture of the organization takes a significant hit. When you think about this topic from a system-wide perspective, you start to see that this kind of turnover will have a huge impact on the culture and finances of the entire Health System."

"We estimate that there could be up to eight CEO and other Health System executive retirements in our system over the next five to seven years. You do the math at a cost of $5.6 million per exiting CEO. And that is why we need to develop and train all of you in this room, with the purpose and expectation that most of you will become the leaders we need for tomorrow."

Sean let that point settle in before he continued, "The plan is for us to meet as a group three times throughout the next year for two full days at a time. Each time we meet, we will work on developing new business and leadership skills. In between the meetings, we will have conference calls to check in on the progress everyone is making and to learn some additional skills. In addition, I will have individual calls with each of you whenever needed."

Maria, whom Sean thought might have been making some progress, yelled out, as if making a joke, "You mean, so you can babysit us?"

Sean was not pleased with the interruption and was reminded that there was still a long way to go with Maria. He wondered if there was someone in the group that he could recruit to help.

While contemplating this question in the back of his mind, Sean continued on with his explanation: "Here are the three things I will bring to this process to help each person in this room develop. First, a commitment to educate you on the business and leadership skills needed to be successful. Second, I will hold each one of you accountable for doing what you say you are going to do in order to develop the skills needed to succeed. And, finally, I will be very candid with you regarding feedback. It is better you hear it from me than to go out there and make a mistake that could have been preventable."

"In return, this is what I expect from you. First, you must put forth the effort to improve. If you do not put forth the effort, you will be asked to leave the program and not be invited back. Second, as a leader, you will be expected to live to a higher standard of behavior both in your professional and personal lives. Any violation of our Code of Conduct Policy & Procedure will also get you excused from this group. Last, we need to be open and honest with each other because that is the only way we will grow and develop. So I expect you all to be open to giving and receiving candid feedback. The time we spend together needs to be in a safe environment where we can take chances and be willing to fail in order to learn and grow."

The intensity of the situation began to sink into each member of the program. Sean picked up a pile of sharpened pencils and lined them up together by tapping them on the surface of the table and said, "So, before we begin, is there anybody here who cannot or will not live up to those three guiding principles for our program?" Sean waited for what seemed like an hour but was likely more like a minute for anyone to respond.

Finally, hearing no objections, Sean said, "Okay, then. Let's get to work."

11

THE CAREER TRIANGLE

S EAN KNEW THAT looking at his watch was not going to change the situation but he did it anyway. It was 7:40 AM and he was already feeling anxious about a meeting he was about to have with Mike Polaski, mainly because Mike was ten minutes late. Before yesterday's session had ended, Sean pulled Mike aside and asked if he'd be willing to meet with Sean today. He wanted to take Mike into his confidence and ask him his opinion on Maria Smith and to ask him to be a "go to" person that Sean could send Maria to if she needed any help. Sean was concerned that since Maria did not fit the definition of a true "high potential" that she could have a negative impact on the dynamics of the group and the overall development goals of the group as well.

Sean had arrived at the Admiral on the Lake by 7:30 AM on this Friday morning at the agreed upon time he and Mike were to meet. He had chosen to sit outside in a beautiful courtyard under a wooden cupola where Sean could tell by the fresh cuts in the wood that the structure had been recently completed. Sean was admiring the detail that the new owners had designed into this facility, down to the bench he was sitting on, which matched the light wood of the cupola.

Sean had at first hesitated at even thinking about requesting Mike's help because he wasn't sure if Maria would benefit from or accept such help. The other potential problem was that asking a member of the newly formed group to help another at such an early stage could backfire if Mike and Maria did not relate to each other very well. Sean decided to take the risk given what he knew about Mike's background. Mike was a "local kid" who had been successful throughout his life. He had grown up in a traditional Polish household where his parents developed a strong work ethic in all of their children. Throughout his schooling, Mike was a straight A student and was also a three-letter athlete at St. Ignatius High School. He had a sport for every season like most of his friends: football in the fall, basketball in the winter, and baseball in the spring. Football was his favorite, a sport that enabled him to get a full scholarship to St. Norbert's College in De Pere, Wisconsin. Mike was the third generation of Polaski's to attend St. Norbert's, all started by his grandfather who attended back in 1959.

While at St. Norbert's, Mike met a beautiful young woman named Sara Campbell who eventually became Mike's wife. It was on their graduation day that Mike proposed to Sara, having asked her father the night before if he could marry his daughter. Sara was from upstate Pennsylvania, where she came from a hard working family much like Mike's family. Happily, both families got along really well, and the engagement just added to the celebration of the graduation weekend.

When Mike returned to Chicago, he got a job in the finance department of St. Roberta Hospital. Within the first year in the new job, Mike and Sara got married, and Mike got his first promotion to Accounting Supervisor. It seemed from there that Mike's career just kept on going straight up, with him moving from the accounting department into the role of Director of Radiology. Mike decided he needed additional education in order to advance his career so he took advantage of the hospital's generous continuing education program to get his MBA in Health Administration at the University of Chicago on nights and weekends.

After graduation, Mike was promoted to be the VP for Strategic Planning, where he was responsible for developing the strategic plan for the next five to ten years for the hospital. Mike was in that role for six years, during which time the hospital added a cardiac surgery program as well as a new Neonatal Intensive Care unit to care for premature new born babies. Because of Mike's solid financial and planning skills, he was promoted to be COO of St. Roberta's and he had been in that role for the past five years. Mike was also held in high regard by many throughout the Health System and recently got appointed to the Health System Ethics Committee. In fact, Sean remembered how it was Mike's strong showing at a recent Ethics Committee meeting that had helped him to be selected as part of the Succession and Leadership Development group.

Mike's career goal was to become a hospital CEO, hopefully at St. Roberta's, though Sean had expressed to Mike that it might be better to get some career experience outside of St. Roberta's instead. As Sean liked to say, "Each organization is different, and getting different experiences helps to further develop the skills needed to advance in one's career."

Mike and Sara had three children, all girls, ranging in age from three to nine. Their youngest child, Emma, was the daughter with Autism. Although it was challenging at times since Emma had severe symptoms that made it hard for her to communicate and engage with others around her, Sara and Mike adored her and made every accommodation needed to help their little girl be an integral part of the family. They were also fortunate to live near a school that could provide Emma with both the educational and social support needed. The school was quite expensive, which made it a constant struggle for the family to pay its monthly bills, but Mike was hoping an eventual promotion into a CEO role would help address the family's financial challenges. At the same time, Sara often regretted moving into their current neighborhood because of the pressure the big mortgage placed on the family. But Mike wanted to live in an area that had some local prestige as his proud mother always used to say to him when he was a child, "Mike, someday you are going to grow up and be so successful that you will live in a mansion." His current home would have made his mother, who had died of cancer three years ago, proud.

Sara and Mike were heavily involved in their local community as well as in their local parish. Sara would volunteer for most of the school activities, and she particularly liked helping her daughters with their Girl Scout crafts, cookie sales, and camping trips. Mike was on the parish finance committee and also enjoyed coaching his children's sports teams.

Sean looked up from his reverie about Mike to see the man himself walking out to the courtyard. It was 7:50 AM, and Mike arrived looking like he had just rolled out of bed. His hair was not combed, his shirt looked like it just came out of the dryer, and to add insult to injury his zipper was down.

Sean stared at Mike in disbelief and asked why he was so late—which was so unlike Mike—to which he responded, "One of our children was sick all night and my wife and I were up most of the night."

"Well, we won't have enough time to discuss what I was hoping to talk about," Sean said, "but maybe we can talk later in the day." As they walked into the main building together, Sean was beginning to have second thoughts about asking Mike to help out with Maria.

* * *

Today's conference room was on the tenth floor and opened up onto a beautiful garden patio overlooking Lake Michigan. Sean knew from his research on adult learners that the more engaged the individuals became, the greater their chances of getting something positive out of this program. So as

Sean stood in front of the room with the beautiful artwork created by local artists, he asked, "So what do you want to accomplish today?"

The question surprised many, and as a result, Sean got some playful responses like "go sailing on the Lake" and "go shopping." Hearing nothing particularly serious from the group, he gave them an assignment. "I want each of you to write down what it is you want out of this program so I and you will know whether or not this will have been a success." With that brief introduction, Sean picked up his smartphone and set the timer for thirty minutes. He then walked around the room and let each person choose a blank sheet of colored paper from his hands and a black marker to use for their brainstorm.

Some started scribbling right away; others sat looking out the window or at the artwork on the walls. Jim Piper and Blake Jones chatted quietly, smiled at each other, and then turned to their own papers. After the thirty minutes had passed, Sean asked for some feedback. Many of the responses were the same. Donna Reuss offered, "I want to develop what it takes to be a successful Hospital Executive. Tom Flowers, DO, added, "I'm looking forward to honest feedback that will help me grow since that has been a missing piece in my career development." This somewhat surprised Sean because although he agreed that candid feedback was essential to growth, he was not quite sure how many of the individuals would react to receiving candid feedback or even whether they'd have the courage to give it.

Sean noticed Maria in the corner of the room, head down, scanning through some text or images on her cell phone. "Maria," Sean asked. "Would you be willing to tell us about one of your own goals for this program?"

Maria looked up from her phone with the briefest look of guilt, as if she'd been caught doing something wrong, but anger quickly eclipsed it. "Damn him," she thought. "He's calling me out because I was added to this group as an afterthought." In fact, Sean wanted Maria to know that spacing out or catching up on emails during program meetings was not an option.

"I'm here for one reason," Maria answered defiantly, "to make sure you clowns are not wasting the systems' limited resources." Neither Sean nor the group could tell if Maria was kidding or was serious, so no one called her out on this comment. Sean smiled, thinking, "I guess we still have a ways to go with this new candid feedback approach." For most of the morning, as the group sorted through their goals for the program, Sean took notes and promised to email a list to them that they could return to in six months and then a year to gauge their progress and success. Then he continued on with the rest of the morning's material.

"How many of you have health insurance?" Sean asked. All of the group members' hands went up. "How many of you have life insurance?' All of the hands went up again. "How many of you have a financial plan?" All but two raised their hands. Tom Flowers, DO, said, "I hate to admit it, but I need to find a financial planner who can help me with developing a plan for our family."

Sister Jeannie added, "My financial plan is in God's hands." This comment got a huge laugh from the group.

"How many of you have a Pension Plan?" Sean continued. All hands went up, including Sister Jeannie's hand. "Last question, how many of you have a career plan?" Only two hands went up: those of Maria Smith and Mike Polaski. Sean then specified, "A *written* career plan," and Mike lowered his hand while Maria kept her hand up.

"So let me get this straight," Sean said. "For most of you, you have a plan for many of the important aspects in your life, including your health, your life, your finances, and your retirement, but only one has a written plan for the economic engine that is going to make all of those plans a reality?!" There was a deep silence amongst the group.

Finally, Blake Jones spoke up. "What does having a career plan have to do with the Health System's Succession Planning efforts?"

Sean said, "Glad you asked that very important question, sir. As we develop the Succession Plan for the Health System, you need to have a career plan that will give you goals in order to monitor your success in this program. Although some folks on high may worry that formulating personalized career goals will take you away from this organization, I have no doubt that many of your career goals will ultimately mesh well with the needs of our Health System. It's funny how that works, but it does. And finally I believe if we are going to lead others as executives, we need to begin 'leading' ourselves by having a plan that will advance our careers and develop our skills so we can become successful."

Kylene Knight replied first, saying, "I never thought about how important it is to lead ourselves before we can lead others. That makes a lot of sense."

"Ladies and gentlemen, do not leave your careers to chance," said Sean. The next fifteen to twenty years of your life are going to go so fast that you will feel you blinked your eyes and everything passed in a blur. Believe me, you do not want to be near the end of your career and say, 'I wish I would have done more' or 'I wish I would have done something different.' Now is the time to lay out your plans. How else will you be able to effectively execute? Having a written career plan will give you something to shoot for and also help you to know what skills and experiences you will need to get to the next level. Do not leave things to chance."

Sean could not help but notice one of the paintings on the conference room wall was of the famous Chicago Harbor Lighthouse and wondered if others in the room caught the symbolism of the Lighthouse painting and how it could be seen as representing the clarity and guidance that a career plan could provide amid life's challenges. Sean continued, "Now I realize a career plan can change depending on life events and experiences, but believe me when I say that you will be much better off changing an existing plan then having no plan at all."

Mike Polaski spoke next in a gentle voice. "I started creating a career plan several years ago when talking to one of my mentors, and it has helped me to realize not only where I want to go with my career but also what skills and education I needed to move forward. My career plan highlighted that I needed to get my MBA sooner rather than later. In fact, since I completed my MBA, I received a promotion from Director of Radiology to VP to now COO at St. Roberta's. I'm grateful for that."

Sean reengaged and said, "Mike, that is exactly what a career plan should do as we begin to map out where we want to go with our careers. Our goal for the remainder of the morning is for each of you to develop your own career plan. As you will see on the sheet that is being handed out, there are several parts to developing a career plan. Before we begin, please write your name at the top so it reads something like, "Tom Flowers' Career Plan" or "Donna Reuss's Career Plan." As each member of the group received a copy of the handout, they saw a picture of a blank triangle with four levels carved into it.

"This is what I call the Career Triangle," Sean explained. "Let's begin at the bottom. You will notice that the foundation of the triangle is split into two sections. In the section on the left, please write in the word *PASSION*. Why? Because I want you to identify your professional passions. This is important because your passions are the energy source that will keep you motivated to do the hard work that is required to do these demanding jobs. In the right side of the bottom section, please write the word *VALUES*. Your values are the GPS instrument that will make sure you stay true to yourself and not be tempted to go off and do something stupid. Believe me, the temptation to do something wrong increases the higher you go in your careers."

Sister Jeannie added, "I love the analogue of the GPS, but I must admit that is not something we have in the convent." This comment got a big laugh from the group and even Maria cracked a smile.

"Now label this level of the pyramid with the word *WHO* on the outside of the pyramid," Sean continued. "This level of passions and values relates to who you are as a person and as a leader." Sean could tell that some in the group were unsure or surprised to begin this planning effort with values and passions so he added, "An important building must be constructed on a strong foundation and so too must your careers."

Sean continued, "Divide the level above your passions and values into four smaller sections, and this is where you will write your professional, personal, and mental or spiritual goals. It is important to identify your goals in each of these areas because each section is important, but also remember that they impact one another. It will do you and the Health System no good if you are a big success professionally and a failure in your physical or personal lives. Eventually, those failures will find a way to seep into the other areas."

Kylene asked, "So what are the four areas again? Professional, personal, physical and... the last one I missed." It was Rachel Pepper, MD, who added, "The fourth section is mental and spiritual."

"This level relates to where you want to go over the next five to ten years in the four main components of your life so I want you to write in capital letters *WHERE* on the outside of the pyramid."

Sean waited a minute or two to make sure that everyone had completed taking whatever notes they needed to help finish this section.

Mike Polaski had the urge to share with the group although he felt a bit nervous. Remembering the ground rules by which everyone in the room had agreed to keep their dealings confidential, he decided to speak. "I already realize I need to do a better job with trying to achieve balance in my life. Work is taking about sixty hours a week of my time, and sometimes I realize I'm not doing enough at home to help out my wife with our three children. I probably need to get back into the gym, too, to help lose some of the weight I gained over the past six years. It would probably help me reduce job stress as well."

Sean just smiled and said, "Now you are beginning to get it. Mike, you will be no good to your wife and kids if you are successful at work but your health is destroyed by your job. It is all about balance. And believe me, it took me many years and bad experiences to learn what I just shared with you. Learn it now, and you will save yourself a tremendous amount of pain and suffering in the years to come."

Sean then continued, "Once you have identified your goals in the four areas of professional, personal, physical, and mental/spiritual, I want you to move to the *next level* of the triangle and identify what skills you will need to achieve these goals. An example could be that to advance in your career, you may need additional education like Mike had mentioned earlier. Some may need to develop new skills to learn how to physically take better care of themselves, like eating healthier, learning how to exercise properly to avoid injury, or getting more sleep. Outside of this level of the pyramid, I want you to write in big capital letters the word *HOW*. Identifying the skills needed to succeed will be how you are going to move from one part of your career to the next."

Again, Sean waited for these points to settle in before moving to the last part of the plan. He gazed out at Lake Michigan and smiled as he saw all of the sail boats crisscrossing their way on the lake on this beautiful late August day. After a moment, he continued, "Once you have described your passions and values, identified the goals for the four important parts of your life, and highlighted the skills you need to develop in order to achieve your goals, it's time to look at the *results* you want to achieve and be known for in your career. With each successful result you achieve, you move up a "rung of the ladder" of success. That's the top part of the Career Triangle."

"For example, if you set as a professional goal becoming a CEO by the age of forty-five or you set as a physical goal that you will run your first marathon by two years from now, this is where you will record your accomplishments, say become a hospital COO before becoming a CEO or training twelve months before running your first marathon. Like we did with the other levels, please write outside of the results section the word *WHAT*. Leaders are known for and get promoted for *what* they produce. This entire process is geared to help you produce the results that will make you and eventually our Health System successful."

Sister Jeannie asked, "I now get the need for a career plan, but how will these plans help the Health System with its Succession Plan?"

Sean thought for brief moment and said, "In order to be truly successful in your careers, you need to be in positions and organizations that will challenge you, compensate you, and be aligned with your passions and values. Having your career plan will help both you and the Health System determine whether, if a particular position becomes available, it will be the right position for you. The worst thing for you and the Health System is for you to be in a job that is not right for you or one that you do not like. Unfortunately this happens way too often."

Sean then asked for each individual to take the rest of the morning to work on his or her career plans. Sean left a drawing of a blank career triangle at the front of the room in case anyone had any questions.

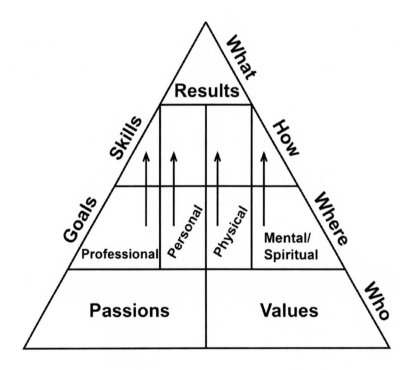

Some of the team members went out on the patio while others went into smaller conference rooms to work on their plans. Sean could not help but notice that all of the conference rooms were of comparable style and décor.

Sean spent some time looking at each of the paintings and thought what a clever idea to feature local artists who were also residents living in the Admiral.

The rest of the morning was quiet as the group worked on their plans. Sean thought, "A little self-reflection and thinking time is a good thing since these leaders are so busy that they almost never get a chance to think about important things like their futures. Many of the great leaders of the past spent time just thinking in order to create new things or to solve critical problems. We all need to do more of that today."

* * *

Since the weather was so nice, Sean had made arrangements with the staff at the Admiral for the team to have lunch on the patio outside of the conference room. The group asked and Sean agreed to hold the afternoon session out on the patio as long as they remained focused on the work at hand. Tom Flowers asked if they could have wine and beer served during the afternoon session to which Sean responded with gusto, "Hell no."

After the lunch plates were cleared, Sean then asked each member to share with the group what they had developed for their respective career plans. Then, Maria's cell phone rang, and without hesitating she answered it. She began a discussion with whoever was on the other line until thirteen sets of eyes focused directly on her, causing her to pick up on the hint that she was disturbing the group. She quietly ended the conversation, without apologizing to the group.

Sean resumed the afternoon session by asking for volunteers to share their career plans, with other members of the group providing feedback. The group felt a little uncomfortable with sharing their career plans since they felt like they would be sharing personal information with others they barely knew. Finally, Harry Klein volunteered to share his career plan. As it turned out, Harry was a great person to begin the assignment because he did a good job of being really "human" with sharing his values, passions, goals, and needed skills, as well as the results he wanted to see in five to ten years. The group really got a charge out of Harry's goal in his personal life to become a championship ice fisherman. This drew all sorts of comments from the group, which also seemed to lighten up the mood somewhat. This was important to Sean because he knew the cohesiveness of this group would be key to its overall success.

After Harry warmed up the group, others became excited to share their career plans. There was some mild push back on some career plans, mostly from others who felt an individual was not thinking big enough about what they could accomplish. It was like the group was beginning to encourage one another to grow either faster or farther, by asking for more clarity. Sean even noticed Maria Smith chiming in with some feedback, some of which was very insightful. For example, when Rachel Pepper, MD, shared how she wanted to be a hospital CEO one day, Maria offered how important it would be for Rachel to really develop her finance skills. Maria added, "Often, physicians will speak as if they know what they are talking about when it comes to financial matters when their knowledge is only superficial. That won't cut it at the executive level. You have to know your numbers." Maria added, "A physician who really knows finance can go far in this world of healthcare reform."

Rachel asked, "How does someone like myself develop that type of financial knowledge?" to which Maria said, "Two things. Find a good financial mentor and practice, practice, practice."

After Rachel was done sharing her plan, Maria went next. The group was pleasantly surprised at how well thought out her plan was and that her ultimate goal was to become a CFO for a large health system. Still, many of them knew of Maria's reputation as being cold and calculating and not someone who had values and passions. A few of them, like Cheryl Butler and Jim Piper, worried that this lack of strong interpersonal skills would make it difficult for Maria to ever achieve her goal of becoming CFO.

As the afternoon of Day 2 was nearing its end, Sean closed with one of the mainstays of this process: "I want each of you to identify two things to put on your to-do list to get accomplished before our next meeting. First, I want you to accomplish something big as it relates to your current job. Second, I want you to accomplish something that relates to your career plan." Sean wanted each member to begin to focus on accomplishing two major goals between each meeting as a way of helping the group establish priorities.

Sean already knew that many members of the group were suffering from what most executives struggle with: having too many priorities and not getting anything meaningful done. Sean had discovered early in his career the same thing, where most young executives try to accomplish too much and actually accomplish little. Sean hoped that by encouraging the group to accomplish just two to-do items, they would begin to see the value of getting focused instead of biting off too much.

After getting the group to think about accomplishing just a couple of to-do items at a time, Sean panned out to help the group see how small accomplishments could add up to big developments over time. To highlight his message, Sean asked the group to think about their professional resume and to consider that if they accomplished just three major priorities per year over five years, they would have fifteen huge accomplishments to highlight as career successes over that five-year period.

Donna Reuss added, "So what you are saying is if I stop trying to do ten things at one time and just try to get three major things done in one year, I will be more successful." Before Sean could answer, Maria added, "Yes, you will."

Sean's closing lesson seemed to work with the group as they all committed to focus on accomplishing two to-do items relevant to their job and careers before the next meeting. Everyone also agreed to complete their Career Triangle and check in with each other to see if anyone needed any additional assistance.

Before Sean called an end to the first full day of meeting with this group, he could see some members beginning to reach out and talk to others in the group. This was a good sign and would be integral to the success of the Succession Planning Leadership Development efforts of the system.

In spite of this general tone of cooperation, Sean could tell that everyone was tired and ready to leave from two intense days of work when he said, "We have one more important thing to do before we leave today." This caught everyone's attention since they were all still new to this process and not sure what to expect.

He continued, "We need to come up with a name for this group as I for one do not believe that 'Succession and Leadership Development Group' works."

It was Jim Piper who said, "And I thought I was the only one who didn't like that name." For the next fifteen minutes, group members called out a variety of names for consideration, some quite funny.

Kylene Knight suggested the "Holy Baker's Dozen" since there were thirteen members in the group, while Tom Flowers added "the Misfits," which drew a few laughs. Finally, Mike Polaski offered the name, "The Futures Academy." There was no reaction to Mike's suggestion other than a few "ah's" so finally Sean asked Mike to explain how he came up with that name. Mike explained, "Given the challenges our system and our individual hospitals are facing, we are a small percentage of the present but we will be 100% of our future."

The group unanimously agreed.

12

THE LEADERSHIP EQUATION

IT WAS THE second week in November, and ice was just beginning to form on Lake Michigan, the only one of the five Great Lakes of North America located entirely within the United States. It had been three months since the last meeting of the Futures Academy, and things seemed to be progressing nicely. In between meetings, Sean had either met with or spoken with each member of the group every month. The monthly conference calls were also well attended; with each thirty days that passed, members seemed to become more involved in the process, sharing more not only about their follow-up items but also asking for help or advice from one another.

Today's meeting of the Futures Academy was being held at the famous Metropolitan Club, located on the sixty-sixth and sixty-seventh floors of the Willis Tower. Before the meeting, Sean looked up some of the history of this famous building and learned that Construction on the original building, the Sears Tower, began in 1970 and took three years to complete. The final structure stood 110 floors tall and cost more than $175 million to build. Originally built as the corporate headquarters for the Sears Roebuck Company, it was purchased by the Willis Holding Company in 1988, a global insurance broker that calls the Tower its Midwest home.

Sean again thought it was a good idea to have these meetings outside of the Health System to allow the group members to really disconnect for a while and not be disturbed by regular work distractions. The first day of the meeting was an "accountability day" where all members had to report out on the items they committed to follow up on since the first meeting. Sean wanted this practice to become a staple of this group as a way of not only helping them get better at holding people accountable (as they would need to do as effective leaders) but also as a way to get each individual comfortable with giving candid feedback.

Admittedly, the candid feedback was slow to develop, but it got a "shot in the arm" when Kylene pushed back on Maria for not completing one of her assignments related to the Career Triangle from the first meeting. Maria did not complete the mental/spiritual aspect of the assignment, which she blew off by saying, "That fluffy part of the triangle is completely unnecessary." Kylene spoke rather sternly to Maria, saying, "None of the assignment was optional, Maria." It was clear that Maria did not like being called to task by Kylene, but unlike times in the past, Maria decided not to push this situation, knowing she was wrong and outnumbered.

As group members reported on their efforts to complete the Career Triangle and complete one major priority between meetings, Sean was impressed with some of the things that had gotten accomplished. For example, Rachel reported that she had successfully "recruited" away from a competitor three orthopedic surgeons who were now already responsible for seventy-five additional surgeries over the past three months. Maria added that she was developing a plan to refinance the Health System's long-term debt in order to get a lower interest rate and reduce costs. Kylene mentioned that as a result of completing her Career Plan, she and her team had begun to develop the skills needed for their hospital to receive Magnet Status, which is a national recognition of Nursing Excellence. Mike added that he successfully completed the negotiations for a state of the art MRI machine. Mike shared that his negotiation skills were tested but he "eventually got the company to agree to 'his terms.'" Tom Flowers added, "I know that strengthening your financial skills is part of your Career Development plan so are you sure you got all of your figures straight?" Everyone seemed to enjoy this jab, even Mike.

Finally, Jim shared how the HR department at Nativity had switched their employee health insurance from a defined "benefit" program to a defined "contribution" program. This was modeled after what many organizations had done with their pension plans years ago, in which the hospital would now contribute a certain amount of dollars to each employee to "purchase" their health insurance on their own. The intent of this move was to get the employees to become more engaged in the purchasing of and administration of their health insurance. The initial feedback from the employees had been positive, and more employees had enrolled in weight-loss and smoking-cessation classes, to help reduce what they paid for their health insurance. This last example generated a great deal of discussion from the group, much of which resulted in others wanting to know how they could possibly effect such a change at their own hospital.

* * *

In contrast to the festive end to the evening where they all enjoy a great dinner at the famous Metropolitan Club, the next day began as overcast and rainy, and the weather seemed to affect the mood of the whole group. Sean sensed they were all a little "flat," so he decided to get everyone involved right from the beginning of the meeting. Sean's instructions were to form four smaller groups and each group needed to develop an equation made up of

all the different traits that they believed were needed for a leader to be successful. Sean drew out the following on the whiteboard:

_____ + _____ + _____ = **Effective Leader**

"We'll call it the Leadership Equation," Sean said, "because if a leader follows it, he or she will be able to be an effective leader in whatever position they hold within an organization." Sean went on to explain that there was an orderly progression as to how a leader develops a relationship with his or her organization just like a salesperson develops a relationship with every customer. Sean went on to discuss the importance of sales skills for every leader. He highlighted how leaders are always "selling" something, whether it's a vision for the future or a new employee health insurance program. "The problem," Sean said, "is that leaders have never been taught in school or in life how to sell something." Sean asked each team to report what they felt were the required aspects a leader needed to become a successful "sales person." Sean could tell by the looks on their faces that the team members had never considered themselves "sales people" but that reality was beginning to sink in.

As they were breaking up into their groups, Blake asked, "How many parts of the equations are there?" to which Sean responded, "As many as you think."

Cheryl Butler asked if Sean would at least provide part of the answer he was looking for to get them started, which drew the following response: "Nothing of meaning in life is ever handed to somebody. Putting in the work and finding the answer by oneself is more than half the battle."

Realizing that Sean was not going to hand any answers to them, the groups went inward and took the rest of the morning to talk through their thoughts on what the different components of a persuasive and effective leader were.

Finally, Sean gave the five-minute warning and asked the groups to finalize their own version of a Leadership Equation, which they would share with the rest of the Futures Academy after lunch. Sean explained, however, that there would be a twist. To communicate their particular Leadership Equation to the others in the room, each team would use the easel and paper to draw symbols that represented their suggested components of the Leadership Equation. Others in the room would have to guess at what was meant. Again, citing the research about how adults learn best, Sean wanted to get the group physically involved in order to get the most out of this exercise.

"This will just be like the game Pictionary, and in our convent everyone wants to be on my team," said Sister Jeannie. Mike responded, upon hearing this announcement from the good Sister, "Can we make a trade in order to get Sister Jeannie our team?"

After lunch, Sean asked, "Who would like to go first?" It did not take long for the group of Maria, Jim, Blake, and Kylene to volunteer. Maria was the spokesperson for the group, and she began calmly and confidently with the following. "We feel there are three parts to the Leadership Equation. First, one must have strong *research* to back up any decision. Second, there should be a strong, *centralized decision making process* that everyone knows and must follow. Third, given all the changes in our economy, there must be an authoritative communication style that lets everyone know, 'You either follow these rules or else.'" Maria stepped away from the easel and revealed what the group had discretely drawn during the morning's brainstorm: a microscope to represent research; a building that represented the Health System offices to represent strong centralized decision making, which got some catcalls from the other members of the group; and a man banging his shoe on a podium, which at first no one understood.

Finally, it was Sean who asked, "Is that last symbol supposed to represent President Khrushchev during his famous speech to the United Nations during the 1960's?" The former Russian president had taken off his shoe while making a point and pounded the podium with his shoe.

Maria, who was a history buff, answered, "That is exactly who we wanted to represent this last point."

Sean added, "Most people under the age of fifty may not know of that famous incident."

Maria just gave a small, smug smile, seeming to indicate that she made no apology for being better read than some of her counterparts in the group. She turned to her team members and high-fived them; it seemed as if this first team felt like they had "nailed" this assignment.

"Any questions?" Maria concluded, almost rhetorically. There was a pause before anyone spoke.

Finally Mike added, "Though I feel your team made some valid points, I don't believe that either successful salespeople or busy executives need to lead with fear and intimidation." Those not in the first group all seemed to agree.

Sean let the tension stand for a moment and then moved on, wanting to give the room time to continue working through the equation. Finally, Sean asked, "Who would like to go next?"

The second group consisted of Mike, Jim, Cheryl, and Tom. Cheryl mentioned how they had struggled with the assignment. After a lengthy discussion the entire Futures Academy realized this team's effort was poor at best. Sean even thought to himself how so far this assignment was not getting the results he had hoped since both teams went with the "negative" aspects of successful salespeople and leaders. Sean then realized how much of the negative slant might be due to the leadership style of the Health System leaders like Miles Greene, Tina Blake, Steve Driver, and Charles Brown, who had limited and authoritarian communication styles and had clearly been rewarded for it over the years. Sean's hopes for success were not very high when the last group stood to present their plan for success.

Rachel was the spokesperson for her group, which consisted of Donna, Simon, Jane, Mike, and Sister Jeannie began with a calm yet confident delivery that caught everyone's attention. Sean happened to look around the room and noticed how many individuals were actually leaning in to hear what she had to say. Rachel explained, "We feel there are four parts to the Leadership Equation." The first image was that of the Statue of Liberty. Maria asked who drew that because whoever it was had some talent. It was Mike, who it turned out had loved drawing since his youth.

Rachel continued, "Like the Statue of Liberty," first, a leader needs to be

VISIBLE

to be successful. Successful salespeople remain in contact with customers even when the customer is not in the 'buying mode.' The same is true for leaders in that they need to be visible so their employees and customers know who the leader is. You cannot run a hospital or a department sitting behind your desk. If you are responsible for an organization like a hospital, you need to be seen on all three shifts and weekends because those employees are just as important as the day shift on weekdays."

"Doctors in particular notice and talk about when leaders are seen making rounds on the off shifts since for doctors that is just part of the job. For example, our group felt that Steve Driver, the CHRO for the Health System, is never visible and that is why no one will take seriously anything that comes out under his signature." The last thing Rachel said about visibility was "In order for the employees, physicians, and volunteers to begin to accept you, they must see you. Many in our group were raised by mothers who said, 'Out of sight, out of mind.' We think that applies for the leader and his people as well."

After a short pause to let the first point sink in, Rachel continued, revealing a picture of a father reading a bedtime story to his young child. Again the detail was amazing with the young child looking directly in the father's eyes believing every word that was said. Mike particularly enjoyed drawing that picture as it reminded him of the time he spent with his kids reading them stories before bed on Sunday evenings.

"Next," Rachel continued, "there is

CREDIBILITY

which for our team means the leader needs to be believable. The key point here is that if a leader says something and then it comes true, then more people will begin to believe and have a little faith in what that leader says about the future. The opposite is too often true. When a leader says something and then it does not happen, the leader loses tremendous credibility." It was Harry who yelled, Mike, if you ever get bored with your day job, you have a career as a visual graphic artist."

Rachel shared a story that helped drive this point home. "Several years ago, our new CEO at the time, David Shulkin, MD, made a commitment to the Medical Staff that the hospital was going to invest $7 million dollars to upgrade the Operating Suite at St. Mary's Hospital. Similar promises had been made by previous CEOs and never fulfilled. In fact, many physicians were placing bets on how quickly Dr. Shulkin was going to backtrack from his bold commitment. To Dr. Shulkin's credit, he delivered on his promise and the Operating Suite was upgraded; as a result, his stock with the medical staff and the employees began to rise almost as soon as the renovations were completed."

Harry added, "Man, we could use more of that around our Health System. Not many believe anything that comes out of the corporate offices."

Rachel continued, with Mike's next symbol, which depicted a young child learning how to ride a two-wheel bike without training wheels. The parent just let go of the bicycle and the child was beginning to ride without any assistance. This symbol had a caption coming from the parent: "Keep going, Johnny. Trust me, you can do this." The look on the child's face showed a combination of fear and excitement. Again, Donna's artistic talents really captured the message Rachel was delivering.

"The third part of our equation is

INTEGRITY

which basically means to be an effective salesperson or a leader, you need to have people's trust. They need to see you as having integrity. Integrity is built upon visibility and credibility. Once people get to know who you are and they begin to believe the things you say, they begin to trust that what you say will come true. This is especially important for a leader as they begin to develop a vision for the future. A vision for the future is about where the Leader wants to take or move the organization. Getting people to buy into that vision will only happen if they know who you are and believe in what you say. Only then will they put their "faith" in what you say will come true. When this begins to happen, people will give the leader the benefit of the doubt, but only because of trust."

As Rachel explained, she continued to use the example of their CEO, David Shulkin. "About one year into his new role as CEO, Dr. Shulkin created a new vision for St. Mary's, which was to become an outpatient organization with inpatient capacity." Dr. Shulkin knew that in the wake of healthcare reform, his organization had to stop relying on filling inpatient beds in order to survive. At first, most of the medical staff and the Board were skeptical but because Dr. Shulkin was visible, people began to accept him. They also were willing to trust him with this new vision. Rachel added, "Dr. Shulkin felt the move to more outpatient services was the right move, and three years later 70% of our total revenue now comes from outpatient services, and our net operating margin increased to 8% last year." Most of the team was not aware of the success that was occurring at St. Mary's mainly because of all the attention focused on those hospitals that were losing money. Upon hearing of this huge positive change, many in the group were blown away with surprise.

Rachel took a drink of her Hazelnut Macchiato coffee since she was getting a little dry from talking for the past thirty minutes. Even Sean thought about how fast those past thirty minutes had gone. Rachel resumed by sharing the last symbols Mike had drawn, which were the classic "happy and sad" faces associated with the theatre, plus a mirror. One face was smiling, while the other was frowning with a small tear in one eye.

Rachel continued, "The last component of our Leadership Equation is

AUTHENTICITY

For us, Authenticity means that the leader can be themselves and not some pretend image or stuffed shirt or skirt that cannot relate to others. Too many times, leaders will put on a pretend charade because that is what they think is expected of a leader or because their ego gets in the way. True leaders are self-confident enough to be themselves, warts and all. In fact, we believe others want to be led by people who are just like everyone else, with triumphs and struggles.

At first, the group did not get the purpose of the mirror until Donna spoke up. "Some of you may not know this, but my husband and I are big fans of the theatre. The reason for the mirror is to highlight how each person needs to look into a mirror in order to see their true self. There is an old saying in the theatre world, "The mirror does not lie." It was Tom, who quipped, "Hell, my parents have been saying that to me for years."

Sean spoke next. "Most executives have a hard time with this last part because they feel vulnerable if employees get to see them as just being themselves. The shame of this thinking is that those leaders would become even more effective if they only became more authentic."

Rachel asked her team if they had anything else to add, and they said she had covered all of their main points. After hearing that, Rachel walked over to the symbols Mike had drawn and said, "For our team, the sum of

**Visibility + Credibility + Integrity + Authenticity
= The Leadership Equation."**

Rachel smiled confidently and asked the group, "How'd we do?"

"You had me at hello," Kylene yelled, in homage to her favorite movie, "Jerry Maguire."

A few others in the group nodded and murmured with approval. Finally, Cheryl said, "Sean, I believe this last group has nailed this assignment."

"What does everyone else think?" Sean asked.

Kylene said, "I for one learned a tremendous amount from their equation and explanation. I believe I and everyone else will need to see a recap of Rachel's explanation because I am sure I missed some of the points that were made."

Sister Jeannie responded, "I believe I can speak for the rest of our team that most of what was shared we learned from Dr. Pepper." Donna concurred with Sister Jeannie's statement about how most of what was shared originated with the good doctor.

Upon hearing that comment, Cheryl asked Rachel, "I would love to know where you learned what you just shared with the group. I know they don't teach that stuff in medical school." Sean observed that there was an interesting transformation going on right before the team's eyes in terms of Rachel. One of the "knocks" against her during the selection process had been her strong personality and how it might negatively impact the group. But ever since the first meeting when someone questioned Rachel's assertiveness, she had begun to become more approachable and team oriented.

Rachel paused and explained, "I began to learn some of what you just heard over the past eight years from Sean O'Brien." This comment drew everyone's eyes toward Sean, only to find that Sean had a look of surprise and shock, which led to his asking, "How did you learn these things from me when we have never worked together?"

Rachel chuckled and continued, "As a member of the St. Mary's medical staff, I would attend grand rounds at Divine Mercy Hospital almost every week. Yes, I attended those rounds so I could help teach the surgical residents, but also the grand rounds coincided with your monthly Management meetings. I used to sneak in the back of the King Auditorium and listen to your updates and also participate in your quarterly Leadership Journal Club. One audio book you assigned was *Born to Win* by the late Zig Zigler and I have been hooked on the topic ever since."

As Rachel was speaking, Sean tried to figure out how Rachel could have attended so many of the Divine Mercy Management meetings with him not noticing her in the back of the auditorium. He laughed at himself when he thought, "Of course you did not see here sitting in the back. Since you are so near-sighted , you could barely see past the front row."

The other thing that made Sean chuckle was how he was constantly pushed by the former system CEO Miles Greene to cut back on his Leadership Development budget in order to produce a bigger bottom line. Sean fought Greene on this and never did cut this budget because he knew how important developing his leaders was to the future of his hospital. Little did Sean know how his fight for those leadership resources not only helped individuals at Divine Mercy Hospital but also Rachel Pepper. That last thought prompted Sean to think about how he hoped it was not too late for this Futures Academy to develop into the leaders that the System needed and to pay some dividends to help save it.

As some began to break for the day, Sean noticed how Maria was talking to Mike. Sean overheard Maria say to Mike, "I liked what Rachel had to say. It made me realize that I don't have much credibility with the hospital finance departments. How do you think I can develop that more?"

Mike thought for a second and then shared, "One thing you can do is to stop having everyone come to the corporate office to meet you and instead you go out and meet people in the hospitals. That way, you can enhance both your visibility and credibility." Maria thought for a moment, then agreed. "Starting next week," she replied, "That is exactly what I am going to do."

13

A ROOKIE MISTAKE

I‌T WAS 6 PM and Sean had some time to kill before he met a friend at Giordano's for some stuffed pizza and to watch the Bulls game on TV. While he was waiting, he sat on a bench not far from the restaurant and decided to check in with Maryanne Richmond and see how she was doing. It was now almost eight months since Maryanne had assumed the role of CEO of Divine Mercy Hospital, replacing Sean since he "retired" back in May. It was hard to believe what all had happened over those months.

Having Maryanne's private office number was key to knowing if she was in the office or not. If she was there, Maryanne would answer since the caller ID on her end would indicate that it was Sean calling from his cell phone. Maryanne answered after the first ring and jumped right to it. "Okay, Mr. O'Brien. What on earth do I do with this Brown character?" she asked.

Sean was somewhat surprised at Maryanne's question since he was just calling to check in and see how she was doing. "And a good day to you too," Sean said, with a teasing tone in his voice.

"I'm sorry, Sean," Maryanne said. "But Brown is giving me a hard time, and I need help pronto."

Sean could tell this time that her tone sounded different.

Maryanne said, "Seriously, what do I do with him? He has become a major pain in my backside with his relentless efforts to get his way. I'm beginning to feel intimidated and doubt myself. I even started going to daily Mass for some divine intervention. But so far God hasn't sent me an answer—or I have not heard what answer he has been sending."

Sean knew from their previous calls that Maryanne's transition into CEO had been tough with the hospital being off budget through the first 8 months of the year. The pressures from the Health System had been mounting on Maryanne to produce the expected bottom line since the system relied on Divine Mercy to carry much of the losses from the other hospitals. Sean had reassured Maryanne that the financial performance would improve over the remaining five months of the year and if it did not he would tell her where he had "hidden" some reserves to help cover any shortfall. But now it sounded like Brown was adding to Maryanne's heap of stresses.

Sean also knew that Maryanne was a very religious person and that in the past when things got tough for her she turned even more to her religion for answers. Maryanne was someone who always had this inner faith that helped guide her through tough times. She came from a very humble background and yet had incredible potential to be an excellent healthcare executive. Maryanne grew up in Tawas City, Michigan, attended Weber State, and received a nursing degree after receiving a scholarship gift from a local business owner, Cathy Maxwell. It was during the summer between Maryanne's freshman and sophomore year when Cathy learned that Maryanne did not have enough money to return to school. Cathy asked her husband Joe, and they quickly decided to help. The two loved helping people in need and often did such good works with no one knowing that they were behind the generous gestures.

Due to the financial gift from the Maxwell's, Maryanne was able to complete her nursing degree in three and a half years. In turn, because of her 4.0 GPA, Maryanne received a full scholarship from the University of Michigan to get her MBA in Health Administration degree. It was finally at Maryanne's graduation from the University of Michigan that Maryanne asked Cathy and Joe, "Why have you been so good to me over the years?" It was Joe who said, "Many years ago we lost a daughter to leukemia and you remind us of her in so many ways. The money we used to help you was money we had put away years ago for our daughter's college education. We always said there would be an opportunity to use that money to help some child attain a college education, and we were only happy to help you."

Cathy added, "The only thing we ask of you is to make your parents, us, and all of the people from little old Tawas City proud, no matter what you do with your career."

Maryanne moved to Chicago right after getting her MBA to accept a job as an Assistant Nurse Manager at Divine Mercy Hospital. In fact, it was while Sean was making rounds on the night shift that he met Maryanne. He could tell she had something special to offer not only to her patients but also to her colleagues: she had the ability to lead. Over the next seven years, Maryanne's career progressed through the nursing ranks. She was promoted to be the Chief Nursing Officer at Divine Mercy following the retirement of a nursing legend at Divine Mercy.

Maryanne then joined Sean's executive team and became a valuable contributor, from day one. She had a quiet confidence about her that served her well, especially in dealing with difficult physicians. At the time, Maryanne reported directly to the COO for the hospital. They worked very well together for the next five years as did the rest of Sean's executive team. It seemed like Sean's team was on a "good roll" when one day they learned that the COO had had a massive heart attack and died in his sleep at the age of 51. Sean knew he had to do something to get his team back and focused on the work at hand and decided to shake things up. Without asking the Board, he walked into Maryanne's office and said, "I want to promote you to be my COO of Divine Mercy, effective immediately."

Needless to say, Maryanne was shocked and initially said, "I'm not ready for those responsibilities." It took another thirty minutes for Sean to convince Maryanne that most executives are never "ready" for the next big promotion. What seemed to help Maryanne decide to accept Sean's generous offer was his saying, "Yes, your learning curves will oftentimes be going straight up, but I will be there to make sure you do not fall off. I see such potential in you and I believe in you. This will be a chance to further develop that potential."

From that day on, they formed not only a great professional relationship but also a strong personal friendship. Sean and Maryanne trusted one another to the point where they would often say, "Trust is being able to put your back to another person's back and never need to look over your shoulder to see if the other person has your back." That visual image of trust is something that both Maryanne and Sean held as sacred. This was a rare commodity in the executive ranks of most organizations. Sean would also never forget that Maryanne had been very kind and helpful to him as he was dealing with Kate's illness and death; Sean knew she was always there to help if needed.

Now it was his turn to help Maryanne.

As it turned out, Brown, the Chairman of the Divine Mercy Board, was up for reelection to City Council in November and he was in heavy campaign mode. Maryanne reported that Brown was using the hospital facilities and staff to host "community outreach" for the hospital when in reality these functions were political fundraisers. Maryanne was kicking herself for allowing the first such event to happen, as now there seemed to be one every month. "Not only are the events being held on the hospital property," Maryanne explained, "but he is ordering high-end food and setting up valet parking, all at the hospital's expense."

As Maryanne talked, Sean was replaying in his mind how he had first met

Brown and how he had learned to work with the man. It was clear from the start that Brown was out for himself and would use anybody to get what he wanted. Even so, soon after Brown joined the board at Divine Mercy, Sean and Brown reached some type of a standstill "agreement" where Sean would leave Brown alone and Brown would not try to abuse his position on the Board for political gain. It was widely believed by many on Sean's executive team that Sean had some "dirt" on Brown and Brown had something on Sean. Whatever they had on each other seemed to keep Brown in check until now that Sean was no longer the CEO.

Sean tried his best to reassure Maryanne, who he knew held herself to very high standards. "It's okay," he said sincerely and gently. "It was a rookie mistake. We've all been there."

Maryanne replied, "Maybe, but I should have known better."

Sean went on, stating, "When we make such a mistake, take the time to think about what you can learn from such a situation. It will be almost certain the exact or similar situation will occur again and you do not want to make the same mistake twice. Next time he calls for such favors, tell him you have to check with the Corporate Legal counsel and that you will get back to him once that's done."

Maryanne thought for a second and said, "I like that for two reasons. First, it's the right thing to do. Second, it will piss him off when he realizes that he cannot just make one phone call to me and get whatever he wants."

Maryanne took a deep breath and felt some of her anxiety dissipating as she exhaled. "Thank you, Sean, for always being there for me."

"You're welcome. And, remember, everything will be okay."

In truth, Sean wasn't one hundred percent sure that it would, not because he didn't believe in Maryanne but because Brown was such a slime ball. Sean wished he could fight this battle with Brown for Maryanne, but he knew it was her turn to try. He wouldn't interfere with Maryanne's efforts, but he would be sure to keep his ear to the ground on Brown just in case.

Before they ended their call, Sean said, "Now that we addressed your work issues, how are *you* doing?"

"Oh, I'm fine," Maryanne said, "just a little frustrated." Maryanne paused as if she was switching gears from work mode to personal mode and said, "Oh yeah, over the summer, I joined the Sandy Hook Beach Club and last month I met this really neat guy. His name is Frank Davalos, and he's a high school teacher who makes me laugh all the time." Sean listened intently and noticed how Maryanne's voice lit up when she was talking about Frank and how happy she sounded.

"Wow," Sean responded, "Remember just last year when we were talking about your Career Triangle and how you felt you were out of balance with working too much and not having enough joy in your personal life? It sounds like you've been giving more time to that personal side and are enjoying the reward."

"It's true," Maryanne said, with a touch of pride in her voice.

"These jobs can eat you alive," Sean said. "The key to being successful is to have balance between your job and personal, physical, mental, and spiritual aspects of your life. Your personal life will take the first 'hit,' followed by your physical life becoming less and less of a priority. Congratulations on keeping your healthy Career Triangle alive and well. And I look forward to meeting Frank at some point in the near future."

Sean was proud of his Maryanne.

14

GOLD IS IN THE BLIND SPOTS

WHAT WAS I thinking?" thought Sean as he was in his office getting ready for the next meeting of the Futures Academy. The only meeting dates that worked with everybody's calendar were March 18th and 19th, which to some was not a big deal. For others who loved to celebrate St. Patrick's Day, like Sean, the day after St. Patrick's Day was never a good day to work because of the after effects of the parades, the pubs, and the overall merriment. "Let's face it," Sean thought. "Chicagoan's love St. Patty's Day!" In fact, they even dyed the Chicago River green in celebration of this "Holiest of Holy" days. Many in the Chicago area just took the day off. This year, Sean had participated in the festivities later in the day, but then cut out after dinner to prepare for the next day's meeting with the Futures Academy. He had a schedule to keep with getting them all ready for their potential career opportunities; if they did not meet on these dates, they would not have another chance to meet for two more months.

The day was dark, cold, and rainy, which seemed to affect the mood in the room. The Futures Academy was ready to begin right at 8 AM, except for Maria, who arrived ten minutes late. Maria did not look like her normal "professional" self, but Sean did not at first give it much thought.

"The assignment for today," Sean began, "was to identify one personal and one professional failure."

Sean had a sense that this day was going to be a struggle given how flat and tired the group appeared to be.

"Who is willing to share first?" Sean continued.

No one looked directly at Sean for fear that if they locked eyes with him they would be called upon.

"Hmmmm," Sean said. "What's going on today? Everyone seems low on energy."

There was a long pause, and finally Maria spoke up, stating, "I must admit I'm still recovering from celebrating St. Patrick's Day. My husband and I went on the 'Erin Express' bus tour of the most popular bars in Chicago. Let's just say it was big fun yesterday, but today I'm paying the price. In fact, my husband who is far more religious than me, went to church this morning to thank the Baby Jesus and the Black cab driver for getting us home safely last night."

Maria's husband, Dan Jacobs, was a friendly, considerate person who worked as an analyst for a local wealth management firm. Those who knew both Maria and Dan often thought that Dan was "too nice of a guy for Maria." Maria and Dan had been married for two years, and they seemed to be making it work, though there were times when others felt Maria would be condescending to Dan while out in public. Sister Jeannie had met Dan several times, either at work functions or at Church, and she was quite impressed with Dan and his ability to try to see only the good in Maria. One time, Dan confided in Sister Jeannie that "Maria is often very harsh toward men in general. I think that it goes back to her childhood days. But I know she adores me." Sister Jeannie thought Maria was in need of a miracle to be successful in a relationship; maybe Dan was just that guy.

Maria's parents, both Catholic, were divorced when she was just nine years old. The children were also being raised Catholic, mostly at the insistence and effort of Maria's father, Xavier. Unfortunately, Maria's mother, Amy, was verbally abusive to Xavier while they were married. In fact, Amy would often take great pleasure out of the regular public "beat downs" she would hand out toward Xavier. After such an incident, Amy would turn to Maria and say, "Never let a man push you around. *Never!*"

After the divorce, Maria lived with her mother and was raised in Sayville, New York. Maria spent very little time with her father at the behest of her mom, even though he made repeated attempts to be part of his daughter's life. Xavier loved Maria, and he did not want her growing up and treating men like her mother did. But there seemed little that he could do to stop the negative influence. The best that Xavier could do would be to end his conversations with Maria stating, "Maria, you are my daughter for life, and I will always be there for you." After watching Maria go through high school and college with one failed relationship after another, mainly because she treated each guy the way her mother treated her father, Xavier lost control of his emotions and blurted out to Maria, "You may have boyfriends, but you will never have a serious relationship as long as you treat the men in your life like dirt. And that's what you do Maria—you treat them like dirt." It was one of the worst arguments that Maria and her father had ever had. Maria refused to accept her father's calls after this encounter, which just broke his heart. The two had not spoken since.

As for the beginning of this meeting with the Futures Academy, many were somewhat surprised at Maria's openness to share the details of her day of drinking. A few in the room may have celebrated St. Patrick's Day, but they would not share the details as openly as Maria for fear it could hurt their career. Some things just need to remain private, especially when it comes to drinking in excess. Sean thought, "Maria will still have to make some major changes if she ever wants to achieve her goal of becoming a Health System CFO. It just seems like she keeps taking one step forward and then another backward."

After Maria's comment, the room remained silent. Finally, Blake broke the quiet by saying, "I really struggled with the assignment. My problem is not the failures—I came up with more than one failure in each category—but my reluctance to share these experiences with everyone here. I'm afraid I'll appear as a real loser if others hear about some of my screw ups." As Blake spoke, Sean could see there was general agreement from the others in the room based on the number of heads that were nodding.

Tom spoke up and tried to normalize the situation for Blake. "As physicians," Tom said, "we're actually trained to identify our mistakes and then share the case during Morbidity and Mortality Conferences. This is a chance for others to learn from our mistakes and for us to admit we did something wrong that may have hurt or even killed a patient."

This was a powerful admission.

"When we make mistakes in healthcare," Sean interjected, "patients suffer. Sometimes they even die. We don't avoid this truth by hiding from it; we deal with it by being honest and working together to become better."

"So," Sean continued, "how many of you have identified a professional mistake?" Everyone raised their hands. "And a personal mistake?" The group members raised their hands again, though much slower than before. Upon seeing these results, Sean decided to change the assignment. "Let's refocus this assignment on only our professional mistakes. If we have time at the end of the day and anyone wants to share a personal mistake, then that will be strictly voluntary."

The revised game plan was well received by the entire group, with even Sister Jeannie stating, "Thank you, Jesus. My prayers were answered since I did not want to share my embarrassing story from my high school prom." This statement coming from a nun definitely captured everyone's imagination, with Harry adding, "We need to make time to hear that story before we leave today." Everyone got a big laugh out of that exchange, even Sister Jeannie.

"Okay, who's ready to share a professional failure with the group then?" Sean asked. The room remained silent. Sean realized this exercise would make everyone vulnerable, but he also hoped they would see the value soon enough. Sean decided to break the silence and stated, "After you are done sharing one of your failures, I will share with you one of mine."

Finally, Mike offered to share a situation that could have ended badly but that he believed he had managed to turn around to a decent outcome. Mike went on to share that in his role as Chief Operating Officer in a community hospital he was also Chair of the Operating Room Committee. This committee was assigned with making sure the Operation Rooms were run efficiently and also providing the highest level of care to every patient. The Operating Room for St. Roberta Hospital was like most hospitals in that it was the most profitable of any department in the hospital.

"At the committee meeting a few days ago," Mike began, "an issue came up that should not have been mentioned for discussion in a public forum. Our Operating Room Supervisor, Vivian Pierce, brought up an issue involving a prominent orthopedic surgeon who last month was verbally abusive to one of Vivian's operating room nurses. Vivian demanded to know the outcome of the investigation involving this surgeon." The surgeon in question had a reputation for this type of behavior, but because he was one of the top admitters to the hospital, Mike explained, everyone historically "looked the other way."

"Four months ago there was a similar situation where this same orthopedic surgeon screamed at a nurse for handing him the wrong instrument. That investigation yielded no punishments to the surgeon and thus a great deal of resentment on the part of the Operating room nurses for failing to address a bad situation." Mike continued, "I responded to Vivian that the issue had been investigated and that this time appropriate follow-up actions had been completed. Vivian apparently did not like my response and pushed her inquiry further, demanding to know what the 'appropriate follow-up action' was so she could tell the nurse in question and the rest of the Operating Room staff. I did not feel this was the proper time or place to have this discussion so I said, 'The hospital has addressed the situation and it should not happen again.'

Vivian reacted with, 'That was the same thing that was said after the last situation, and four months later we have a similar situation with the same surgeon! I tried to discuss this with you in private but you kept ignoring my requests.' It was at that moment that I began to take this exchange somewhat personally and said, 'We are not going to discuss this topic anymore. Consider this case closed.'"

Well, that response did not sit well with Vivian, who responded, 'Mike, you have always been fair in the past, but in this situation, I feel you are putting the bottom line of the hospital ahead of how we treat our employees.' I'll be honest…I got mad at that statement and said, 'Vivian, this is none of your goddamn business and now I'm going to ask that you leave this meeting.' Vivian looked shocked at my response and left the meeting in tears. As she was leaving the room, she shared with me and the rest of the committee the following: 'Because of the way this situation was handled, the nurse who was involved resigned this morning because she knew nothing else was going to happen with this surgeon.'"

There was stunned silence in the room at what they just heard about how this situation was handled by "one of their own." That being said, many in the room could see how an unexpected situation could just spiral out of control.

"I just felt I had to try and control the situation before it got really out of hand," Mike added in a quiet voice.

Finally, Donna asked, "If you had to do it over again, what would you do differently?" Mike responded after taking a moment to think, "I am not sure what I would do given the difficult situation—given the history and circumstances. I think I actually handled this well. All I can hope for is that Vivian will calm down and eventually be okay with how things unfolded." Mike was always known as a very fair and principled person, yet it seemed like the more he spoke, the worse the situation got.

Sean now knew this could go one of two ways. Either no one would challenge Mike, or they would all gang up on him. If they all ganged up on Mike, then the whole reason for this exercise would be compromised since no one would go next and share their own "failure" story.

Finally, Sister Jeannie spoke. "I believe you could have handled this situation in a very different way, Mike. First, Vivian was trying to meet with you prior to the meeting. Could you have made it a priority to connect with her? This type of discussion is always better handled in private—even you said it shouldn't be mentioned in a public forum—and yet it sounds like Vivian was unable to get your ear."

Jim waited for the right moment and added, "The behavior of that surgeon was totally unacceptable. He should be thrown off of the hospital medical staff. I do not care how much value he brings to the hospital, keeping a clown like that around will do you more harm than good."

Sister Jeannie added, "Amen to that!"

Jim continued, "I'm also reminded that we have as our corporate values 'Integrity, Respect, and Excellence,' and I feel you did not live up to those values in this situation. This surgeon obviously did not respect the nurse in question and also had little respect for the hospital in the way he behaved. And in displaying such behavior, he lost all integrity or, as Sean educated us earlier, the ability of others to *trust* him. The result now is that one talented nurse has resigned and you will be lucky if Vivian stays since now she has been publically humiliated trying to right a wrong."

At this point, Mike began to realize how he had not only misread this situation but also how poorly he had handled this situation. To his defense, Mike said, "I now feel like I screwed up, but it was one of those situations where I was not prepared as to how to handle it. How can I turn things around?"

Tom offered some thoughts. "Mike, I believe we all need to lead by example, and I suggest you first apologize to Vivian in private. Second, reconsider the game plan with the surgeon and give serious consideration to some type of appropriate discipline that would also send a signal to all of your employees and medical staff that such behavior will not be tolerated. Last, I suggest you reconvene the Operating Room Committee and apologize for how this situation was handled. Do not wait until the next meeting because this situation will just fester until you address it. It takes a courageous leader to admit when they have made a mistake, and I believe you will learn and also teach a valuable lesson to all those who were involved in this situation by accepting some fault."

As Mike looked around the room, he could tell that others agreed with Tom, Sister Jeannie, and Jim about how this situation could have been better handled and also what to do next.

Mike responded, "I appreciate your feedback. And even though it hurts to admit I did something wrong, it is also a great benefit to have this group to share such an experience with and learn from your collective feedback." That last comment from Mike was actually a "gift" to Sean, which might help with what he was about to offer to the group.

"I want to thank Mike for sharing his situation," Sean said, "and being brave and vulnerable enough to share his 'failure' so both he and all of us can learn from this situation."

"Happy to be the guinea pig," Mike said with a slight smile, his cheeks blushing.

"Mike," Sean said, "know that one of the greatest teaching tools we have at our disposal is in fact our 'failures' and being open to learning when something does not go well. Too often we do not take enough risks because we are afraid of failing. And then when something goes wrong, we race to correct it, try to forget it, and quickly move on to the next thing. But our mistakes are such a valuable opportunity to learn. A mistake or failure may or may not define your career, but it will always define your character. In fact, how you handle a mistake or failure is more important than how you handle a success.

It will speak volumes as to the type of person you are, and it will help you bounce back rather than flounder."

Cheryl volunteered, "My family never discussed failures. In fact, they went out of their way to either distance themselves from a failure or they made every effort to hide any and all failures."

"The main lesson here has to do with our blind spots." Sean could tell he just entered into a conversation that got the attention of the group just by the way they all seemed to lean into the center of the room to hear more.

Sean continued, "We all have blind spots where we think we are right, and yet if we have someone who knows us and is honest with us, they can help to point things out where we are wrong. Many times, when such a point is brought to our attention, we fight it, but after further reflection we realize the other person is right and we are wrong. The saying, 'The gold is in the blind spots' highlights what great learning and development opportunities exist as long as we are open to being exposed to our blind spots." The concept of a blind spot seemed to resonate with most of the group except for Mike, who pulled his smart phone out of his pocket and started scanning newly received emails. Mike's lack of focus aside, a lively discussion ensued about how many in the room were not even aware of their blind spots.

As Sean paused, Mike suddenly tuned back into the discussion as if something he heard had finally caught his ear. His whole body language changed, and he spoke back up, stating, "I know I really struggled with this exercise, but now that I am on the other side of it, I must say it was really helpful. Thank you for giving me a safe environment where I could tell my story and get real-time feedback. It's something I have never experienced before. Oftentimes, I try to figure things out on my own, but now I see the value of talking things through with others I trust and whose opinion I value."

Unfortunately, there was something else nagging at Mike—some decisions he had made in the past six months that this conversation was causing him to start to question. Yet, given the gravity of these decisions, he knew that he couldn't say anything to the group and would just have to figure out this other situation on his own.

With that, Donna said, "I'll go next." For the next several hours, each individual in the group got to share one of their failures and receive very valuable feedback from the rest of the group to help understand why things had unfolded as they had and how the person could have handled things differently.

The group stayed almost thirty minutes past the ending time of the meeting when Tom yelled out, "Hey Sister Jeannie, how about telling us that prom story now?" Sister Jeannie turned a slight shade of red and responded, "Not in a million years."

* * *

The meeting on the second day was filled with the "accountability" updates from each member of the group. Sean was pleased with the updates and highlighted accomplishments. It appeared the group was more focused and achieving greater results than ever. The other benefit was the group's comfort level with providing candid feedback to one another, a trait that would serve them all well in the future.

Sean never ceased to be amazed at how individuals could develop when given the formal opportunity to reflect and receive feedback. He wished that he had had more candid feedback in his own life, especially when it came to personal issues. He certainly could have benefited from someone like Frank Hetherton earlier in his life, before he made the ultimate mistake that pushed Kate into her drinking.

Talk about personal failures. Sean wondered what the Futures Academy would think of him if they knew the truth about him and Kate. But before he could beat himself up too much, he could hear Frank's voice in his head asking him if Kate had forgiven him. Sean knew she had and was finally starting to understand that he also had to forgive himself in order to begin to move forward with the rest of his life. Holding on to all of the Irish Catholic guilt and pain was causing more harm than good. He couldn't change the past, but he could certainly do his best to positively affect the future.

15

DECIDE OR DON'T DECIDE

S EAN LOOKED AT the clock on his office wall when his cell phone rang
at 6:45 AM. Who could be calling so early? It was two months since
the last meeting with the Futures Academy and he was supposed
to have a monthly phone check-in with them in an hour. Surely, it wasn't
someone from the group as they would be set up on a video conference line,
not dialing Sean directly.

It was Maryanne Richmond.

"Hi Sean, am I catching you at home?" Maryanne asked into the phone.
"I'm sorry for calling so early."

"No problem, Maryanne. I'm already at the office," Sean replied. "With
this great weather, I got up a little early and jogged here. Gotta get my exercise," Sean finished. It was the middle of May, and spring was just starting to
bloom in Chicago. Sean was enjoying the change in season.

It had been several weeks since Sean and Maryanne had last spoken, and
Sean had a sense from the early timing of this call that it was not going to
go well from the start.

Maryanne launched, "Brown's been calling me at all hours of the day and night—and not to wish me happy birthday either. Surprise, surprise, he's come up with some more favors to request of me."

Once Maryanne paused, Sean jumped in and added, "By the way, happy birthday. Is this your 29th?"

Maryanne caught Sean's joke and said, "All of my birthdays from here on out will be my 29th!"

Having said that, Maryanne launched right back in on Brown. "Ever since Brown won reelection, he has been a pain in my backside. This time, he is asking for a physician friend to be given special Operating Room Block time."

Sean commented, "He must be trying to repay a debt he has from the election."

"As you well know," Maryanne continued, "the Operating Room block time is reserved for those surgeons who are loyal to the Hospital. Giving a surgeon a block of four hours of Operating Room time is something to be earned and not given away as a political gift."

Sean could tell that Maryanne was beginning to feel more comfortable in her new CEO role. In the past two months, the hospital had made up significant financial ground, and it now looked like they would make their budgeted bottom line for the fiscal year. This fact alone had taken a great deal of pressure off of Maryanne and her team, especially from the Health System leadership who counted on Divine Mercy to produce a healthy bottom line. The financial results had turned around due to some "laser focused" expense management and also some new patient volume coming from several key physician recruitments by Maryanne over the past six months. In addition to the improved financial results, Maryanne had made some key leadership changes that had sent a signal to the rest of the organization that everyone needed to produce or they would not be promoted. Some of the changes involved leaders who were loyal to Sean but became too complacent and figured "tenure was more important than talent." Maryanne knew changes needed to be made and was gaining confidence with each successful accomplishment. Sean could sense she was still struggling with how to handle Charles Brown, though, the ever challenging politician and Board Chair of Divine Mercy Hospital.

Born and raised in Chicago, Charles Brown began his career in the trucking business utilizing some of his family connections. After barely graduating from college, Charles wanted to follow in his father's footsteps and work in a union shop. Charles' father, Hank Brown, had been in the unions for years and had an attitude that the union should get whatever it could to benefit its members while also doing anything it could to screw the employers. Hank's motto toward the trucking company was "God Bless me and the hell with you!" He passed that motto and work ethic on to his son. Charles followed in his father's footsteps quite nicely.

Charles' reputation grew when he got involved in an effort to unionize a small, local trucking company that had never been unionized. The CEO of Sunrise Trucking had always been good to the company employees over the years but financially could not match the wages and benefit upgrades the union employees were receiving at other unionized companies. Hank Brown knew it would be difficult to unionize the Sunrise Trucking Company so he had Charles apply for and get hired at the firm as a loading dock employee. The strategy was for Charles to gain the confidence of the other employees and then start to advocate from the inside for a union.

Charles was only on the job four months when he saw an opportunity arise, and he took it with great energy. Charles' job was now to make life a "living hell" for the management of the company, and he became quite successful at causing work productivity to fall while raising the anger amongst the non-union employees at what their union counterparts were getting paid. There were reports of equipment damage and even some workers' homes being vandalized late at night. The tension within the company rose almost daily, culminating in Charles leading a "wildcat strike" that resulted in the Sunrise Company being shut down for five days. After an all-night negotiation session in which Charles had participated, an agreement was reached whereby the Sunrise workers would become unionized and receive immediate, unbudgeted salary and benefit increases in return for ending the strike. It was not until the signing ceremony of the new union contract that the Sunrise Trucking CEO learned that Charles was Hank Brown's son. The owner was overheard asking the VP of HR, "Who the hell hired Hank Brown's son?"

After the effort to successfully unionize the Sunrise Trucking Company, Charles' stock rose within the ranks of the trucking union and also politically within the city. Eventually, Charles won a large seat on the Chicago City Council, which was notorious for political patronage. Charles' reputation also began to grow outside the City of Chicago with the trucking union using his presence and tactics to help with other unionizing efforts in other states. Charles had been warned by many to be careful with his activities so as not to draw the attention of the local FBI. This was one reason why some speculated Charles was spending so much time outside of Illinois.

Sean was brought back to the situation at hand when Maryanne was heard saying, "I cannot grant Brown his request to give some surgeon valuable OR block time when the surgeon is not even very active at our hospital."

Sean cleared his throat, preparing to respond, but Maryanne continued. "Sean, I'm concerned Brown will ruin the hospital and possibly my career with these requests."

Sean regrouped and said firmly but kindly, "Maryanne, just because the Board Chair makes such a request does not mean you have to honor it. As you know, there is a process for how OR block time is evaluated and granted. You need to allow the existing process in place to run its course. Just refer the issue to the OR committee and then call Brown to let him know the steps his request will take. In fact, you should be proactive and call his office to let him know what the next steps will be. You and I both know he is a coward and will not take the call so you can leave a message with his wonderful assistant, Joanne Downing. That Joanne is a wonderful person and I often wonder how someone so nice could ever work for a man like Brown."

* * *

"As leaders, we are known for the decisions we make and the results that those decisions produce," Sean said after welcoming the Futures Academy to the video conference call. "The challenge with making decisions is that the higher you go in an organization, the fewer decisions you will make, but the greater the impact they will have—on the organization and your career. So today we are going to discuss how to make better decisions."

Before Sean could continue, Sister Jeannie spoke up and reminded Sean that the conference call had begun without saying a prayer. Feeling somewhat embarrassed, Sean asked Sister Jeannie to lead the group in one.

After the prayer, Sean launched into the actual assignment by asking, "So how do you make a decision?" This question seemed somewhat basic, and yet there was no one willing to share their decision-making process.

Finally, Jim Piper offered, "After listening to the problem, I tune into my gut and pay attention to what it's telling me to do."

Sean added, "So Jim, what are the steps you use to make a decision?"

Jim paused, having never fully thought through the process before. "I guess I never really think about how I make decisions; I just make them," he said.

Sean could not have asked for a better answer to help support his reason for having this discussion. Sean asked the rest of the group, "Does everybody do basically what Jim does when it comes to making decisions?" The general response was the same—"yes"—with Maria specifying, "I do what Jim does, but by the way you are asking the question, I am beginning to assume we should be doing more than we are doing."

155

Sean was pleased to see that Maria was engaging in this discussion and said, "The first thing we need to do before making a decision is *fully understand what the problem is*. The successful executives of today and tomorrow will be known just as much for identifying the problems as for solving them. You need to think about spending at least 50% of the time toward understanding that problem before doing anything else."

"Oftentimes, we assume that we understand the problem after only spending a brief amount of time thinking about what the problem is and then we launch into some solution. But when this happens, we will often attempt to solve something that is not actually the main problem. In fact, we will oftentimes solve a *symptom* of the problem rather than the true reason for the problem itself."

Kylene asked, "What process should we use to fully understand the problem?"

Sean smiled and said, "What I have found really helpful is to ask the question 'why' five times."

Kylene countered and said, "Can you give us an example?"

Sean searched for an idea and then recalled a story he had hoped to share with the group. "I will use a real-life example that helped me to learn this process. The Blaber family from our home state was visiting our nation's capital, Washington DC, while on spring break. Arriving at the famed Lincoln Memorial, they learned, however, that the site was closed. The inquisitive father, Reg, went up to the National Park ranger stationed outside of the Memorial and asked, "Why is the Memorial closed?" The young Ranger, named Ada, responded, "The Memorial is closed for cleaning," to which Reg asked a follow-up question. "It's odd that such a popular Memorial would be closed for cleaning. Why does it need to be cleaned?" Reg asked.

Ada smiled and said, "The Memorial is being cleaned because of dirt from pigeon droppings."

Reg thought for a moment and asked a third question. "Why is the

Memorial such a popular place for the pigeons?" Ada did not hesitate and said, "The pigeons are attracted to the spiders that are popular around the Memorial." Now Reg was on a roll and asked his fourth question. "Why is the Memorial such a popular place for spiders that results in the problem of having to clean up excessive pigeon droppings?" The young National Parks ranger, who was well trained and did not appear to be phased by these questions, responded, "The spiders migrate to the Memorial in order to capture enough moths to eat." This last response fully engaged Reg, and now his two anxious teenage daughters were getting embarrassed that their father was asking so many questions. But Reg persisted by asking his fifth question: "Why do the moths find the Lincoln Memorial such a suitable place to live?" Ada just smiled, thought for a bit, and then added, "The moths are attracted to the bright lights that illuminate the Memorial."

By now, Reg's wife and two daughters were beginning to walk away when their father thought about the answers to his five questions and then shared the following summary with Ada. "So let me see if I have this straight. If the lighting of the Lincoln Memorial were changed to a type of light that would not attract moths, the spiders would not be attracted to this site, in which case the pigeons would not be here and subsequently the Memorial would not have a problem of pigeon dirt that needs to be cleaned. And if there was no need to clean up the pigeon dirt, then there would be no need to close the Lincoln Memorial for cleaning."

By now, Reg's family was two hundred yards away and was attempting not to even look back at their father trying to solve a problem for the National Park Service. Ada just smiled and said, "Sir, I am going to submit your suggestion to my boss for consideration. In addition to your name sir, I will need your occupation."

The father responded quite proudly, "My name is Reg Blaber, and I'm an electrical engineer. I work for NASA and we had to solve a similar problem when we were scheduling shuttle launches at night. It took us nearly nine months to solve this problem so I know that if you change the type of lights being used, you will save big money from not having to clean up after all of those pigeons. Because of our experience with trying to solve a moth problem, we at NASA now use the 'ask the why question five times' as part of our standard operating procedure when dealing with simple and complex problems."

As Sean paused for effect, Donna jumped in and said, "It was a shame that Reg never got to see the Lincoln Memorial up close."

Jokes aside, the example provided by Sean seemed to make sense and really drove the first part of problem solving—and decision-making—home to the group.

"So because they didn't understand what the problem really was at the Lincoln Memorial," Mike clarified, "they had to keep shutting it down for periodic cleaning."

It was Tom Flowers who said with a sense of confidence and understanding, "So once you ask the why question five times, you have your answer to the problem—the right answer to the right problem."

"Not so fast," Sean answered. "Many people will assume they have the right answer to the problem, but it's still not time."

Maria Smith added, "That would be moving too fast. There must be a Step 2. You need to identify several options to consider as *possible solutions* to solving the problem."

"Right," Sean continued, "you don't assume you have the one right solution. You consider multiple solutions."

The group seemed to reel a bit from the fact that Maria had just answered Sean's question correctly. Then Mike said with conviction, "Nice, Maria."

Sean jumped in and asked, "So how many options?"

Maria answered, "At least three, maybe as many as five."

"That's right, Maria. Now who can tell me what Step 3 should be?"

Tom Flowers asked to speak next and said, "Now that we have all of our options on the table, we need to begin to research them."

"Excellent," Sean said. "But why is research so important?"

Tom continued, "Because we need to give each option a chance to survive and not be excluded out of hand. I have found some people will shoot down a good idea either because it sounds odd or because it was not one of their own suggested options."

Sean asked what the group thought of Jim's Step 3, and Cheryl answered first. "I didn't even think about research, but now that I think about it, that makes great sense. I used to work with a boss who would often shoot an idea down because his ego would always get in the way. It would make us all crazy because sometimes the ideas were really good, but we weren't able to execute any of them because the boss hadn't thought of them himself."

After Cheryl finished her comment, Harry added, "Research is also important because when a final decision is reached and someone asks you to defend your decision, you will have greater credibility if you can reference outside research."

Everyone agreed with this step, and finally Donna said, "I could have used this with a recent decision I made that turned out to be wrong mainly because I only considered one option, and if honest I did not do any research to support my decision. I just went with my gut."

Sean jumped in, "Good, now what is Step 4?" Sister Jeannie spoke next with a tone of voice that seemed to sound more like a question than a statement. "Next, I believe we would need to narrow the options down to the final two. Right?" There was no immediate reaction to Sister Jeannie's comment, and finally she asked the group why there was no response. At almost the same time, several spoke up and admitted, "We're trying to write all of the steps down so we don't miss anything." Those comments made Sean feel good that this was the right topic at the right time for this group.

"I agree with Sister Jeannie," said Kylene. "It just makes logical sense that after you identify the options and conduct your research, it's time to narrow your choices."

Sean sensed he needed to pick up the pace of this lesson in order to get it in under the allotted time for the conference call so he simply said, "Yes, Sister Jeannie and Kylene are right about Step 4. How about Step 5?"

The group wanted to go right into making a decision between the final two options, but Sean kept on saying "No, you are missing some steps." More suggestions were made, and finally Harry spoke about adding something from the Vatican.

Jim added, "How do you propose that helps to make good decisions?"

Harry said, "When the Catholic Church is considering a candidate for Sainthood, it appoints someone to argue *against* this decision. The position of the Devil's Advocate forces those involved to think through all sides of the issue, which results in making better, more informed decisions. So in our situation, a Devil's Advocate will ask questions and try to present information that goes against a recommended course of action."

Once Harry finished, there was silence for close to sixty seconds when finally Rachel spoke and said, "I love that suggestion. I say it should stay." Everyone agreed quite quickly.

Finally, Rachel added, "If I ever need a Devil's Advocate, I want Maria to be one for me."

Maria just smiled and said, "I guess that role can come easy to me at times." There was muted laughter. Sean suspected that if the group were meeting in person, they would have known Maria was trying to be funny with that last statement.

"Okay, keep going," Sean said. "We have four important steps left. Who can identify them?"

Simon Gratz said rather dismissively, "How many steps does it take to make a decision?"

Sean couldn't tell if Simon was getting impatient or simply surprised.

Blake Jones said, "I believe the logical next step would be to make a final selection from the remaining two options, choosing whichever will best solve the original problem. And I would think that would do it—but there is more?"

Sean nodded and waited. The quizzical looks on many of the faces indicated to Sean that they were not sure what else was left. No one spoke. Finally, Sean added, "Before you implement your decision, it must pass the 'ethics test.'"

"Okay, I'll bite," said Mike, inviting Sean to share more. As a member of the Ethics Committee, he was often having to think through the tough issues of this topic. Plus, due to some of his recent choices, the question of right and wrong had been on Mike's mind a little more than usual.

Sean was happy to respond to Mike's comment. "I learned about the ethics test from one of my mentors, Andy Sullivan, an insurance executive," Sean explained. "Andy explained that before any major decision, he would always think about the decision in terms of whether he could look his children and wife in the eyes and explain his reasoning for making this particular decision. Andy felt that if he could do that, then it was an ethical decision to make."

Just then, a computerized voice came on the conference call, reminding everyone that the call would end in five minutes.

"Wait!" said Cheryl. "Hurry up and tell us the last steps of the process!"

Jim spoke up and said, "As the Human Resources guy, I got this. Once the decision is made you have to *communicate* the decision to all interested parties. Often, a great decision is made but then poorly implemented because it was not properly communicated."

Sean loved the way that Jim described Step 8 and replied, "I could not have said it better myself. Now you are ready to implement your decision— Step 9. Making decisions without taking action is a huge waste of time and effort, and yet it occurs all the time. You have to follow through on your decision—to execute—for this process to have positive results."

Before the call ended, Sean said, "Let's have a different member of the group quickly highlight each step of the decision making process." As they did, Sean wrote down what they each said on a whiteboard, which he pointed his WebCam onto so the group could see the steps clearly. By the time the Futures Academy was done sharing and Sean was done writing, the following list appeared for all to see.

Step 1: Spend fifty percent of the time trying to understand the problem.

Step 2: Develop three to five possible solutions to solve the problem.

Step 3: Research each option and include others in this process.

Step 4: Narrow the number of options down to two.

Step 5: Appoint a "devil's advocate" to argue the opposite side of each option and try to prove each right.

Step 6: Make a decision between the final two choices.

Step 7: Perform the ethics test on your decision.

Step 8: Properly communicate your decision to all interested parties.

Step 9: Take action to fully implement the decision.

Just before the call ended, Sean shared one of his "pearls of wisdom" by saying, "Please keep in mind that when making a big decision, the goal is to be respected, *not* liked. Too many leaders do not want to offend people with their decisions because they want to be liked, but remember that being liked is not the goal, moving the organization forward is."

"You will be respected," Sean continued, "if you follow the steps we just highlighted, you adequately explain your decision to all of the appropriate parties, and you implement your decision."

"Amen!" said Sister Jeannie.

Mike then added, "Hallelujah!"

Sean smiled at their enthusiasm. The video conference call wasn't quite the same as if the team had been meeting in person, but it was darn close.

16

THE UPDATE

I T WAS A warm and sunny June day on the Chicago lakefront when Pat
met Sean outside the main entrance of the Shedd Aquarium. Like a
true gentleman, he had already purchased two half-day passes. Pat had
asked Sean to pick a location for their meeting that would enable them to
talk about the progress of the Futures Academy while also allowing her to see
another highlight of this fine city.

It had been almost ten months since the Futures Academy was commis-
sioned, and Sean wanted to give an accurate status report on how well each
member of the group was progressing. Pat and Sean's original plan was to
have some of the Futures Academy members ready for advancement one year
after the program began. Sean knew some were making progress, but he also
had to admit that no one was ready for immediate "graduation" into a high
executive-level position.

Sean and Pat entered the Aquarium, which from the outside looked like
a large 1960s-style government building with four huge stone pillars in the
front. Since it was just after 9 AM on a Tuesday morning, the crowds were

light, which would enable Pat and Sean to tour the facilities easily while discussing the Futures Academy.

"The Shedd Aquarium was the first inland aquarium with a salt water fish collection," Sean explained to Pat, happy to give a brief history lesson to the newcomer in town. "The aquarium is also known for its 'rainbow' of colorful fish: dolphins, beluga whales, octopus, and Sean Jellies. There are more than 30,000 animals here."

Pat listened intently and said, "Impressive." Sean could not tell by the tone of her voice whether Pat found the Shedd Aquarium impressive or the fact that Sean knew so much about the Aquarium. Or maybe Pat was just trying to be polite.

Either way, Pat quickly moved to the subject at hand, by asking, "So how did you come up with the name of Futures Academy?"

Sean was glad to get this conversation started with an easy question. "Actually, Mike Polaski first brought up the name to highlight how the individuals in the group would represent the future of the Health System leadership."

Pat smiled and said, "I would not have come up with the name, but I definitely like it as well as what it represents for our organization."

Next, Pat asked, "Since you mentioned Polaski, how is 'wonder boy' doing since everyone seems to think he has success written all over him."

Sean and Pat had just entered the Caribbean Reef exhibit when Sean responded, "Mike is making nice progress with his Career Plan Triangle, and he is completing all of the requested assignments. He is also seen as a positive influence on the rest of the group and is encouraging to other members."

"That's good," Pat said as she stopped and commented on how interesting it was to walk around this gigantic fish tank while watching a diver swim in the salt water with all of the thousands of tropical fish.

Sean continued, "Mike's customized Leadership Development Plan is focused on him further enhancing his strategic planning, financial management, and communication skills. He is doing better than most with developing his communication skills, and he is looking for any opportunity to speak in a public setting to gain more experience. The area that is giving Mike the hardest challenge is developing his financial management skills. Mike is making progress, but he is not ready to take the financial management proficiency test anytime soon. With time, he will master the financial management skill, and I believe he could be ready for a CEO role within the system in six to eight months."

Pat paused while watching the diver navigate her way around a large beluga whale. Finally, Pat asked, "Do you think Polaski could be our first success story coming out of the Futures Academy?"

Sean thought for a moment and said, "He could well be, but there is something I want to keep an eye on over the next several months before I firmly commit to that statement. It just seems like over the past several weeks he's been a little distracted and off his normal game." Sean had learned to trust his gut over the years. Although Mike was doing everything asked of him, Sean still wanted to see more before announcing that Mike was ready for his next career opportunity.

Pat added, "If I had three young children and his job, I would be a little distracted myself. Don't stress too much over Mike. In both your career and mine, we weren't ready for our next career move but somehow after we were pushed into a larger role we survived."

Sean laughed and said, "I guess you're right. I'll keep working with Mike to help him prepare."

As Pat and Sean continued to walk, they reviewed the other members of the Futures Academy. Sean shared some particular highlights with Pat, including the great work being done by Jim Piper, CHRO of Nativity Hospital. Jim had been heading up a team of HR leaders from throughout the Health System who were looking for ways to reduce costs. The particular focus of Jim and his group of "merry men and women" had been to consolidate the seventeen different employee health insurance plans down into three plans as Jim had shared in a previous meeting of the Futures Academy. They were putting the final touches on this effort, which would result in annual savings of $6.5 million due to better competitive pricing and fewer administrative costs.

The yet to be quantified benefit to this change was that employees would be incentivized to utilize the Health System hospitals, resulting in increased inpatient and outpatient volumes. Jim even helped develop a communication plan that he and all of the Health System key leaders would use to effectively communicate this decision and its impact on the employees and the Health System in general.

Pat waited until Sean was finished with sharing this good news on Jim when she asked, "Where is Steve Driver in this whole effort to consolidate the employee health insurance plans?"

Sean just chuckled and said, "Driver has been putting this off for years, afraid of alienating some of the employees. So Jim started this work without Driver, but now that it is getting closer to a reality, Driver is reengaging. Convenient timing, as always, for Driver. Some of the hospital CEOs and myself are betting that Driver will try to insert himself into the effort just before the main announcement so he can get some of the credit."

Pat just kept walking and said, "Driver's day will come and it won't be pretty. At least, Jim and his team are doing well. Let's keep challenging Jim to see how he continues to develop."

Pat waited till Sean was finished with the update on Jim and the others when she asked, "I noticed you left Maria Smith for last. How's she doing?"

Sean thought it somewhat interesting for the two of them to be entering the Amazon Rising Flooded Forest when the topic of Maria came up for discussion. Sean began by saying, "On some fronts, Maria is making nice progress, but her personality keeps getting in the way of real progress. She is making strides on her Career Plan Triangle, especially with developing her strategic and quality skills. However, she still seems pretty rough around the edges in terms of how she interacts with people."

Pat did not even wait for Sean to pause when she added, "I have a golden rule that states, '*Never* promote someone who has poor interpersonal skills.' No matter how good they are with other skills, being an executive with poor interpersonal skills always results in bad things happening for the organization."

Sean knew that what Pat was saying was one hundred percent right and just nodded his head.

"Look at Maria's boss, Tina Blake," Pat continued. "That woman is probably one of the smartest healthcare financial minds in the country, and yet her personality is toxic. At some point, she is likely to self-destruct like all other executives who have poor interpersonal skills. I have discussed Tina's dim future with the Board, and they do not want me to make any other changes with the Health System executive team until the new CEO is in place. So for now, unless Tina does something really stupid, we will just have to put up with her. However..."

Sean just smiled and said, "The day when it is announced that Tina Blake departs this organization will be a day that many will stand and applaud."

"As for Maria," Pat resumed, "unless she makes some significant progress with developing her interpersonal skills, she cannot remain part of the Futures Academy." That was exactly what Sean thought Pat was going to say, and yet it made him sad because progress was being made by Maria. He had to figure out how to accelerate her progress in the most difficult skill of the five, her interpersonal skills.

Sean and Pat walked a while when Sean finally spoke again. "I agree, but I want to give her a little more time. Beneath the hard exterior, I am seeing glimpses of some leadership potential. Maria has not had any strong role models throughout her life, and she would definitely benefit from some special mentoring and candid feedback. She is like a bully who everyone is afraid of. Sometimes the 'bully' needs to be punched real hard in the nose by life to let them know they cannot get away with treating others like dirt."

Pat did not hesitate. "Well, then you better hit her hard and fast before she implodes. I do not have to remind you that the Board and many on the System executive team are questioning the purpose and funding of the Future's Academy and they are just waiting for someone like Maria to slip up to be the reason to shut the whole program down."

Sean thought about how, originally, he had not wanted Maria to be part of the Future's program, and now the success or failure of the program might just depend on how well Maria developed.

17

GET UGLY EARLY

IT SEEMED LIKE just as Sean got back to his office and sat down at his desk that he noticed by the caller ID on his phone that Steve Driver was calling. Sean thought about how Steve never called him. "This is going to be interesting," Sean thought.

Sean answered the phone by saying, "Holy Spirit Health System, Futures Academy, this is Sean," when Steve blurted out, "I've got some news for you, friend."

Sean bristled when he heard Steve call him that, knowing that Steve never had and never would consider Sean a friend.

Steve continued, "Sean, it appears that your superstar Mike Polaski will be arrested sometime today."

Sean's eyes widened as he leaned forward in total shock. "On what charges?"

Steve added, "He will be arrested for taking a bribe from a radiology equipment vendor."

Sean listened and then asked, "How was he involved?" He needed more details before he would even consider believing something so preposterous.

Steve went on to say that the FBI had called to make him aware that one of the Health System employees was about to be arrested for taking a bribe. It turns out the person the FBI was investigating was Mike Polaski. Reportedly Mike and the Director of Radiology at St. Roberta's hospital were at the national radiology equipment convention two weeks ago when the bribe offer occurred. Mike had attended this conference for years and still did even though he was now the COO for the hospital. They were being "wined and dined" by an equipment company that St. Roberta's was considering for its new MRI. While out for dinner, the Radiology Director overheard the company sales rep offer Mike $50,000 if his company was the successful bidder for the MRI equipment. What shocked the Director even more was when she overheard Mike say, "I have always come through for you in the past and that amount will work just fine. My CEO trusts me and will accept whatever recommendation I make."

Sean was trying to digest all of this information, and at the same time he could not help but notice a hint of satisfaction in Driver's voice as he was sharing this terrible news with Sean. Sean then asked how this issue came to light.

Steve added, "The Director was so upset but unsure what to do about this obvious violation of the law and our Ethics Policy that she finally reported it to our Ethics hotline, which eventually made its way to me. We immediately turned this over to the authorities given the seriousness of the allegation. I might add that your 'superstar' is a member of the Health System Ethics Committee. A little ironic, don't you think?"

Steve's voice got even quicker when he said, "Sean, as you know I have not been a fan of the Futures Academy, and I would not be surprised if the Board upon hearing about Mike Polaski decides to shut your program down. We both know Charles Brown has also not been a fan of yours or the Futures Academy. In fact, I am sure the *Chicago Tribune* will have a field day with this story, which means a guy like Brown will be looking to take advantage of this crisis. Brown is already mad and promises when he gets back in town to raise 'holy hell' over this incident."

Sean just had to ask, "How does someone like Brown already know about this and I am just finding out now?"

Steve hesitated because he realized that he should not have shared that last part about his calling Brown to let him in on the Polaski investigation. Instead of answering the question, he simply ended the call by saying, "Do not be surprised if this incident results in a big black eye for the Health System and the sudden closure of your beloved Futures Academy."

* * *

Of course, the news of Mike getting arrested had come immediately after Sean had just given Pat Scott a very positive update on how the program was doing.

It took Sean about thirty minutes to find out that Mike had been arrested while at work and was currently at the local police headquarters. Sean was uncertain as to whether he should go and visit Mike. On the one hand, he felt angry that this incident could result in the Futures Academy being closed down, which could make it challenging for him to speak to Mike in a non-heated way. On the other hand, Sean could only imagine how devastated Mike must be right now and knew he could probably benefit from some company. After some consideration, he decided to visit Mike at Police Headquarters.

As it turned out, Sean knew the arresting officer, Kristen Mulvihill, from when Kristen was assigned to the precinct that serviced Divine Mercy Hospital. Sean always made it a priority to have a great relationship with the local police and fire departments. Fifteen years ago, Kristen and Sean organized the first annual "toys for tots" Christmas toy drive for the needy children in the neighborhood.

After shaking hands and getting caught up on Kristen's family, Sean asked,

"So how is my boy doing?" Any anger Sean had felt toward Mike dissipated as soon as he walked into the police station and imagined him sequestered in some room.

Before Kristen responded, she thought, "Typical Sean, always treating those he works with as part of his own family. I guess that is one reason why a guy like Sean is so well liked and successful."

Kristen responded, "He is really shook up. Distraught even. He admitted to the crime and even shared how this was not the first bribe he had taken. In some ways, he almost seemed relieved to be caught, and that is why he has offered additional information to help our case against the company."

Kristen led Sean down the hallway where he could observe Mike sitting in a beat-up old conference room consisting of a metal table, two metal chairs, a wall-mounted trash can, and a two-way mirror on one wall. As Sean was looking through the two-way mirror, he said to Kristen, "That is a good guy in there, a good family man who has made some really stupid mistakes."

After about an hour, Sean learned the bail was set at $200,000, which meant Mike was going to have to post at least 10% to get out of jail today. When Sean went in to meet with Mike, he could not help but notice the smell of vomit in the room. As Sean passed the trash can in the corner of the room, he noticed that in fact Mike must have recently thrown up. Upon seeing Sean, Mike stood and said, "Sorry about the odor in the room, but my nerves got the best of me." Not only had Mike thrown up, but his face was pale white and his eyes were red from crying.

Sean spoke next: "Come on, Mike, it's time to go home."

Mike added, "I can't go home; I can't post bail."

Sean replied, "I already took care of that."

Mike asked, "You did? Why would you do that for me?"

Sean thought for a second and said, "Hey, I have made mistakes in my life and I understand where you are right now. I figure if I can help you in your time of need like others helped me, then that is what I should do."

Sean's tone changed to be more authoritative when he said, "In return for posting your bail, I want to know exactly what happened—without any BS. There is a saying in the military, 'Get ugly early.' I want to know what happened and why." Mike knew Sean was not kidding around so he told him everything. As Mike was talking, Sean was comparing what he was hearing with what Kristen had told him and the stories were identical. The new information that Sean was not aware of was that Mike's family finances were out of control partially due to the added expense of raising a child with a disability and also due to Mike's costly life style. For example, the cost of their daughter's special needs grade school was $24,000 a year, and the mortgage to their house cost more than two-thirds of Mike's pay check.

Mike started crying when he blurted out, "How am I going to explain to my wife and children that I have done something terribly wrong and I may be going to jail?'

Consistent with Sean's style of being blunt, he said, "If you are convicted of the current charges, you will spend some time in jail. But the important thing is to try not to get ahead of yourself and instead to just concentrate on one step at a time. The next step is to get you cleaned up so you can go home and tell your family."

Mike asked, "How will I repay you for posting the bail?"

Sean responded, "First, you have to promise me you will not leave the state of Illinois. Second, remember, one step at a time. Now let's go home to see your family." Mike began to stand and asked Sean again, "Why are you doing this for me?"

Sean smiled and said, "Son, I have made a few bad decisions in my life. I am not here to judge you. Time to go."

Later, when they were in Sean's car, Mike said, "I know I screwed up and I never should have taken that first bribe because after that the others just seemed to be easy. The truth is, my decision-making process was 'blinded' by the need for money, and I convinced myself no one would ever find out. I guess if I had asked a devil's advocate before I made these decisions, I would have probably handled it differently."

"We had the chance to live within our means and I let things get out of control. I was the one who wanted to move to the fancy neighborhood, send our special needs child to a private school and drive the fancy cars. I made poor decisions and now I must pay. I blew it and because of my poor decisions, I will lose my job, my house, and possibly my wife and family. How do I explain this to Sara and the girls?"

Sean, looking straight ahead while driving said, "I guarantee you this will be the hardest conversation you have ever had in your life, but you will get through this. Just be honest with what you say in answering any questions your family will have. This is not the end of your world, but you must face this like a man."

As Mike and Sean entered Mike's house, Mike could tell his wife, Sara, already knew just by the look on her face. His three children were home from school playing like it was a normal day, which indicated that Sara had not told them of the news about their father. Sara could not bring herself to hug Mike. Instead, having noticed his vomit-stained shirt, she went and got him a clean shirt from the laundry room.

After hugging all three children, Sean asked them all to gather around the kitchen table. Mike's oldest daughter, Jordan asked, "Is something wrong because whenever we sit around the kitchen table and it's not meal time, it usually means something is wrong." Sean thought to himself, "Even a child can be perceptive when something bad has happened."

Mike, remembering Sean's counsel from the car ride to be honest, responded to Jordan, "Yes, I have some bad news to share with all of you." To Mike's credit, he shared all of the major points to the story at a level that the children could understand. With each shared detail, Sara cried harder and harder, and at one point their autistic daughter Emma got up and walked over to their mother and said, "It's okay, Mommy, you will be alright." Upon hearing that comment, Sean had to use every bit of reserve to not start crying himself.

Mike's middle daughter, Alyson, did not say a word, but the look on her face was of pure disbelief, like one of her heroes had just been defeated by some bad villain. After Mike was done with his explanation, it was Jordan who asked with tears running down both cheeks, "Daddy, will you be going to jail?" The directness of the question shocked everyone, and Mike said, "Yes, Jordan, I will probably be going to jail to pay for the wrong I have done."

It was at that moment that Sean could no longer hold back his own tears.

18

THE SLIPPERY SLOPE

FORTUNATELY, THE MIKE Polaski scandal did not make the evening newscast, but it would just be a matter of time before the story ran on the media circuit. When Sean finally got in touch with Pat by phone to make sure she heard the true story, and not just Steve Driver's version, Pat asked Sean in a not so friendly tone, "How could one of our superstars get caught up in such a mess? It was just this morning you were telling me about Polaski's upside potential, and then several hours later he is arrested for taking bribes?"

"I wish I could explain this," Sean replied, "but I can't." Sean sounded dejected.

Pat was concerned that the Polaski story would generate renewed interest on the part of the news agencies to put the entire Health System under a microscope again since Miles Greene's having left under a cloud. The scrutiny would be intense and could motivate the Board to take some hasty actions that it would not normally do in calmer times.

Sean's mind flashed back to the time Miles Greene was under investigation, and then he remembered another time when a hospital executive was caught falsifying payroll records. In both situations, the Board agreed to immediately terminate both executives since it wanted to be viewed by all parties as taking these types of situations seriously.

Pat said, "I already got a phone call from Charles Brown requesting a board meeting as soon as he gets back in town. I'm not sure when that will be, but my gut tells me we have less than a week before that meeting occurs. I can only imagine how Brown is stirring the pot with other Board members to further his own interests. In fact, while talking about Polaski, Brown took a shot at Maryanne Richmond and said how uncooperative she had been over the past several months. I took that comment from Brown to mean that Maryanne has actually been doing her job well and standing up to Brown."

Sean paused and then replied, "Knowing Brown, he'll take full advantage of this situation to advance his own agenda and to inflict some damage on others."

Pat said, "My biggest concern is that we were just beginning to make some progress for the Health System and get some momentum going our way. Now this happens, and it could distract us away from the things we need to keep turning this place around." Sean heard in Pat's voice the first hint of doubt since she had arrived in her messy interim role and wondered if Pat was beginning to doubt that she could help "right the ship."

Sean spoke next with an affirming tone: "Pat, please know the positive impact you are having on this Health System. We will figure a way to get through this."

"Why would Mike do this?" Pat asked, as a pained tone came through in her voice.

"I've been asking myself the same thing," Sean said, "because Mike is such a great guy and he cares about the hospital and his work. And his family."

Pat replied, "He has always seemed to me to be a solid person…a real straight shooter."

"I guess even straight shooters can make poor decisions. Mike was using the money from the radiology equipment company to help pay down his large mortgage and to cover his kids' school tuition. It looks like he got in over his head."

"And," Sean added, "the FBI apparently has been tracking the transfer of money from the company to Mike and they can validate Mike's admission that this is not the first time this has happened."

Pat listened and let everything Sean just said sink in. She then added, "I'll be honest, Sean. Mike's not the only one I'm worried about here."

An eerie wash of worry came over Sean, and he felt the same shame and anger he had experienced on the day last May when he had learned that he was being forced to resign from Divine Mercy.

Pat shared that she had heard from two other Board members that Brown was already making calls and drumming up support for not only canceling the Futures Academy but also was asking that Sean be fired over this issue.

Upon hearing Pat say that Brown would take this opportunity to come after him, he asked almost rhetorically, "Why is he coming after me?"

Pat then asked in a more direct fashion, "Isn't now a good time to tell me about your history with Brown?"

Sean suspected that this day was coming between Pat and himself but had hoped by some act of God that it would not be needed. Now he knew he had to have this conversation with her. Sean began rather directly, "For many years, my wife was an alcoholic. During that time, she had many arrests for driving under the influence. But I had great relationships with many of the police officers and their bosses, and the DUI charges just seemed to 'disappear.' Because of my position at the hospital and within the community, I went to great lengths to keep any issues involving her out of the public eye. Brown found out about my arrangement with the police and took full advantage of one particular situation when I was at the police precinct waiting to take Kate home after being picked up for her fourth incident. My cell phone rang, and it was Brown." Sean went on to explain how Brown had shared that he was aware of Sean's wife's predicament, and he would only agree to keep the incident quiet if Sean appointed him to the Hospital Board of Divine Mercy.

Sean continued, "Here I am, trying to keep this whole situation quiet, and Brown not only knows about it but he is also trying to take advantage of the situation. The bottom line was I appointed Brown to the hospital Board as a concerned community citizen, and he agreed in return to keep his knowledge of Kate's alcohol problems quiet."

"Wow," Pat said, letting her guard down momentarily. "How did this happen?" She knew the answer and yet...this wasn't the Sean that she knew.

"Pat, I wanted desperately to keep Kate's troubles quiet. I knew never to accept a deal with the devil, but I felt like I had no other choice. I agreed on the spot to appoint Brown to the Divine Mercy Board. That was six years ago."

Pat was so surprised by what she was hearing as she sorted through it all in her mind. To hear that Sean himself was responsible for putting one of the most corrupt Board members in place was shocking.

Pat continued reflecting on the news from Sean. In both cases, Polaski and Sean had made a decision in their lives that started them on a "slippery slope," which eventually led them both to a bad place. Pat had learned early in her career that some people will make compromises that they deem justified at the time even though they know they go counter to their values or passions. The initial decision is usually something small that they justify in their minds either through the logic of "it won't hurt anybody" or "no one will find out." The sad reality is that once the first bad decision is made and there are no consequences, it makes it easier to make the next bad decision. The next decision is usually more severe than the first, but still the person rationalizes it in his or her own mind as an okay thing to do. This process continues until they are in so deep they fail to see it as a problem or they continue to believe they will never get caught. But just like in the world of gambling, the averages always catch up, and eventually the situation explodes.

Sean could tell that Pat was having trouble making sense of it all, and so after the long period of quiet, he added, "I must admit that I am not proud of what I have done, Pat. It turns out that like Mike, I made a bad decision in order to save my family. But that doesn't make it right. I take full responsibility for my actions."

There was a long pause, and Sean was fearful of what Pat was going to say next. When she finally spoke, she sounded understanding. "I have never been in that position so I really cannot relate, but I believe you did what you thought best for your family."

Sean said almost with a sigh, "Yes, at the time it seemed right, but I am not so sure given what I know now."

"I'm glad you have told me the whole story so we know what we are really dealing with. We will just have to see how this all plays out over the next several days."

Pat was already strategizing on how she could minimize the impact Brown might have on this situation. She made a mental note to call her baby sister Sue to check in on a special project she had asked about several months ago. As she and Sean were getting ready to hang up the phone, Pat said with an ominous tone, "This could get ugly for both of us so we better be prepared for the worst."

* * *

Right after Pat hung up from speaking with Sean, she called her sister, Sue Scott, on her private cell phone and asked what progress had been made on her request for information on Charles Brown. Sue was a 45-year-old FBI agent assigned to the organized crime unit out of Manhattan. One of the things Pat struggled with the most before taking on this interim assignment in Chicago was the idea of being away from her family back in New York. She ultimately decided to proceed, reminding herself that it would be a temporary assignment and that she could call back home often, which she did.

It just so happened that she had a work-related reason to do so shortly after she began her tenure at Holy Spirit. It was soon after Pat took on this assignment that she got the sense that Charles Brown was going to be a problem for the organization. Pat called Sue and asked her to "unofficially" look into Brown's past to see if there was anything going on that might prove to be leverage. Pat knew from years of experience in dealing with politicians that the one thing that could keep them in check was leverage. Leverage could be in many forms, but it had to be something of substance and only to be used selectively. Pat also knew that due to Brown's large presence in the state of Illinois, she would need to get an "outside set of eyes" to look into Brown.

"Have you found anything?" Pat asked her sister once the call got underway.

Sue reported that she had not been able to uncover anything illegal with Brown within the City of Chicago or in the state of Illinois. That was not the feedback that Pat was hoping to hear, especially with the pending board meeting and the problems created by the whole Polaski investigation.

Pat huffed, exhaled, and explained to Sue everything that was going on regarding Mike Polaski. She continued, "The word on the drum is that this fool Brown is going to use this situation to not only close down one of my pet projects but also to try and destroy a career of a healthcare legend in this town."

"So that's what's driving you forward on this," Sue said, piecing everything together.

"That," Pat continued, "and the fact that Brown and some of his cronies on the Health System Board are holding this place back from making some of the important decisions it needs to make in order to move forward. If I can't get Brown and his cronies off of the Board, then this whole organization may crumble in a short amount of time."

"Sue, you have to keep digging," Pat went on. "As Dad used to say, 'Always trust your gut,' and my gut tells me this guy is not clean. I need your help to find something on Brown ASAP."

Sue could hear the desperation in her big sister's voice and added, "I hear you loud and clear. Maybe since Brown is working more with the national trucking union, we'll find something looking into his and the union activities in other states."

Pat responded rather quickly, "Then get on that option. We don't have much time. The board meeting is likely to happen in a couple of days."

What Sue did not share with Pat was that she had already initiated that investigation several weeks ago and that there might just be something there. Sue and her team had noticed that Brown's travel had increased over the past twelve months into Ohio, Indiana, Michigan, and Pennsylvania, which might indicate that he was getting bolder with his unionizing activities. Hopefully, the update Sue would be getting later in the afternoon would shed some additional light on Brown and his union activities.

After Pat hung up, she remembered how as children her sister Sue was the one who worked the hardest in school and was always a fierce competitor when it came to sports. Hopefully, that same discipline and tenacity would help her with finding some useful details on Brown.

19

A New York Second

THE NEXT MORNING, Sean held an emergency conference call with the Futures Academy from the road to discuss everything that seemed to be unfolding with the Polaski incident. He had planned on initiating the conference call from his office at the Wellness Center but was caught in traffic due to some type of accident on Lake Shore Drive that had caused all of the morning traffic to be at a standstill. Except for the ambulance and police trying to make their way through all of the traffic to the accident scene, no other cars were moving.

Once on the conference line with the Futures Academy, Sean took the next ten minutes and shared what he could about Mike. He asked all the members of the group to pray for Mike and his family given the hard times they must be going through at the moment. Sean also knew it would be normal for someone to be thinking Mike was getting just what he had coming to him so Sean added, "It would be easy to judge Mike harshly here, but remember, we are all human, and we all make mistakes. I know this better than most people."

Maria Smith asked a question soon after Sean gave his update. "Is it true the Futures Academy may get closed down because of what Mike did?" There was a tone of real concern in her voice. Sean had anticipated this question, but he did not think it would come from Maria.

Sean paused and then responded, "I cannot lie to you and say the Futures Academy is one hundred percent safe. I have heard rumors that there are some who want to see it shut down. All I know is that there will be a special board meeting on Friday. What I can share with you is that Pat Scott remains very supportive of our Academy, and she and I will continue to support and defend the merits of our efforts with the Board. We cannot control what decisions the Board will make, but we can control what we do with our own Leadership Development Plans and the jobs we are paid to do. I suggest we all stay focused on the goals and priorities at hand."

Soon after the call ended, the traffic congestion started to subside. As Sean replayed the just completed phone call in his mind, he wished he could have shared more with the Futures Academy about what might happen at the upcoming board meeting. The frustrating thing was that Sean did not yet have a clue on how to help the Board see past this isolated incident involving Mike and to focus instead on the merits of this program. He only wished that there were several "graduates" of the program that were already in executive positions that he could point to as real success stories.

Sean was shaken from these thoughts when his cell phone began to ring and he noticed on the caller ID that it was Maria. He wondered for a brief moment why she would be calling him on his cell phone since Maria had never called him on his cell phone in the past.

As Sean answered the phone, he heard Maria yell, "Oh my God. This can't be happening. Please don't let this be happening!" She had a frantic tone in her voice, as if a building had started to collapse and she had to stop it.

"Maria? What's going on?" Sean asked.

Maria started to scream, "My husband was hit by a car while out jogging this morning along Lake Shore Drive."

Sean thought, "Holy shit, that must have been the reason for the traffic jam I was stuck in this morning."

Maria added, "All I know is that an ER nurse from Divine Mercy called my cell and told me about Dan's accident and that he is being evaluated by the trauma team. She said I should get there as quickly as possible."

Sean's mind began to race, knowing that if Dan was being evaluated by the trauma team, then he must be in bad shape.

He asked Maria the following, knowing she would be in no condition to drive: "Where are you now?"

Maria said, "I am in my office at the Health System."

Sean responded, "I want you to walk down to the lobby, and I will make arrangements for one of our security guards to drive you to the hospital."

Before they hung up, Maria said through tears, "Sean, if there is anything you can do to help my Dan, I would be very grateful."

20

I Love You, Let Me
Count the Ways

THE DRIVE TO the hospital took less than ten minutes due to the heavy morning traffic. Sean knew he could park near the emergency room, which would save him time instead of going to the parking garage, which was a hike away. As Sean was getting out of his car, the security guard came charging toward Sean, yelling, "You cannot park there…." As Sean kept walking toward the guard, it then became clear that he recognized who Sean was and then offered, "Sorry to yell like that, Mr. O'Brien, but it has been crazy around here this morning."

As Sean passed the triage area, he was met by the Nursing Director of the Emergency Department. She gave Sean a big hug and then took Sean over to see Dr. Amy Goldberg. Sean got another hug from Amy and realized this was the one thing he missed since he "retired"—the contact with the patients and the staff. As a "people person," that was one part of his job that he never used to tire of.

Amy looked at Sean and said, "We still don't know the extent of Dan's head injuries because he's not back yet from getting the CAT scan. I will say this, though: If this young man was not in such good physical shape, he would be dead by now."

Dr. Goldberg said the medicines he was currently on should stabilize his vital signs and give them time to assess the extent of his other injuries. In addition, Dan had a compound fracture of his right lower leg, which for now had been stabilized. He also had a punctured lung, which had been re-inflated, and he was currently on a ventilator to help with his breathing. The major area of concern was his head injuries. The police officer at the accident scene told Dr. Goldberg that Dan was thrown twenty feet into the area upon impact. The initial impact of Dan's head resulted in a two-inch indentation in the windshield of the car that hit Dan. The initial police report indicated that the car that struck Dan was driven by an 89-year-old man who had apparently become disoriented and ran a red light going at least fifty miles per hour based upon the skid marks at the accident scene.

When Dr. Goldberg finished her "clinical" review of Dan and his condition, Sean then asked, "What are his chances?" to which Dr. Goldberg replied, "The patient is in very serious condition, and the next forty-eight hours will determine his chances of survival."

Sean thought for a moment and then asked, "Should we start talking to the family about making end of life decisions?" Amy could sense the hurt in Sean just by his even asking that question given what Sean had gone through with his wife three short years ago.

Amy responded, "We only offer the patient's family what they can handle so it would be premature at this point to have that conversation given what we know. They must first digest what all has just happened to the patient, and then as things change, we will decide how to handle the end of life and possibly organ donation decisions." That counsel seemed to make sense to Sean. Then Amy asked, "What again is your relationship with the patient?"

Sean explained how the patient's wife, Maria, was in the Health System Leadership Development program called the Futures Academy. "Maria is a very talented financial leader who has some great potential," Sean explained. "We have been working with her on becoming more people oriented, and to her credit she has been making some real progress. Her husband Dan has been a very positive influence in Maria's life too. They have been married for less than two years, but he has been helping Maria change for the better. I am concerned that the injuries to her husband could really set her back in so many ways."

Amy processed what Sean had said about Dan and Maria and added, "I remember when you recruited me here and you were real honest with the then state of the ER department at Divine Mercy and told me, 'There is nothing better in life than come-back victories.' We proved that back then and I believe with your help Maria can also still achieve a similar come-back victory in her life no matter what happens to her husband."

Sean just smiled and then started to tear up a little bit when Amy in an effort to break the mood asked, "Are you still collecting pennies?" This last question caught Sean by surprise until he remembered how Amy was in the room the night before his wife Kate slipped into a coma and the subject of Kate and Sean's penny collecting had come up. The tears suddenly began rolling down Sean's cheeks with the thoughts of his late wife Kate, and then he said, "Yes, I'm still collecting."

Suddenly, a loud voice came from the ER security area. It was Maria yelling at the triage nurse as she and the security guard were trying to walk straight back to see her husband. The Nursing Director was the first to intervene and escorted Maria back into the trauma area where Dr. Goldberg and Sean were waiting. After initial introductions, Dr. Goldberg gave Maria an overview of her husband's injuries, similar to what Sean had just heard. Sean could see that Dr. Goldberg was back in her clinical mode, providing all of the details in a very matter-of-fact way.

Just as Dr. Goldberg was finishing, Dan was wheeled back into the trauma suite, and Maria screamed in shock at his physical presence. Seeing his swollen face, a ventilator, numerous IV tubes, plus a contraption holding his leg straight just overwhelmed Maria. Sean grabbed Maria before she fell to the floor and the Nursing Director secured a chair so Maria could sit down. Sean knew immediately from his earlier conversation with Dr. Goldberg why now would not be a good time to discuss end-of-life organ donation decisions. The last time Maria saw her husband was this morning before work when he was getting ready for his run, and now his body was near destroyed and clinging to life.

* * *

The process of moving Dan up to the Neuro ICU occurred without any problems, and Sean introduced Maria to the Neuro ICU Nurse Manager. The Nurse Manager was very kind and compassionate when speaking with Maria, though she knew that only a small amount of what she was sharing was actually sinking in with Maria at the moment. She finished with, "Our goal at Divine Mercy is to treat every patient as if they are a member of our family," echoing something Sean and Amy had been discussing earlier. "We try to live up to that standard every day and our nurses and physicians will take great care of your husband."

Sean stayed with Maria in the unit throughout the morning and afternoon. During that time, Dan's condition did not change, which was a small positive sign. In truth, however, the news was not good. Dr. Mike Duncan, Chief of Neurosurgery, came by and reiterated that Sean was in serious condition. Surgery might also be needed, and it appeared that Dan might never return to his normal state. Sean could tell some of the events of the day were beginning to sink in with Maria, and yet there were still things that Maria just did not comprehend. For example, Maria said, "When he wakes up," and Sean knew based on what Drs. Goldberg and Duncan were saying that the chances of that happening were slim.

Toward evening time, Sean walked Maria down to the room on the unit where she could go later to sleep or eat a meal. He asked Maria if she needed anything before he departed and if she wanted him to call anybody. Maria explained somewhat guardedly that she had contacted Dan's parents earlier in the afternoon. She was not sure, but she believed they would be arriving late tonight or early tomorrow morning. Maria shared how Dan's mother did not like to fly so they would probably be making the eleven-hour drive from Atlanta. Sean then learned that Dan's parents did not get along with Maria, but felt that now was not the time to ask the specifics of their relationship.

Sean asked about contacting anyone on her side of the family, and Maria said quietly that she had had a falling out with her mother recently and she had not spoken to her father for years. Upon hearing that Maria was basically alone at the present time, Sean added, "It is really hard to go through such a life-changing event without any family or friends. I want you to call me anytime, and I will be there for you."

Maria began to cry as the severity of the situation sank in a little more and said, "Dan is really the only person in the world who gets me, and now I may lose him. Just this morning before leaving for work, Dan was getting ready for his morning run. As he was getting set to leave, he came up behind me to give me a goodbye kiss when I let out this really loud burp. Dan stopped short and said, 'There is nothing in life that says, "I love you, let me count the ways" more than a really loud burp.' We both just laughed and then went about our regular daily routine where he went for a run and I left for work. Not long afterward, he was hit by the car."

Maria's face strained as she tried to hold back tears.

"I want my Dan back. I want things back the way they were this morning. And I want to say I'm sorry for all of the times I treated him badly." The tears came rushing down Maria's cheeks. She cried a deep cry that originates from the soul and only occurs when a life-changing event touches the person crying. Sean knew that type of cry from his own life experiences and just wanted to help anyway he could.

Finally, Sean spoke and reassured Maria, "Dan is getting the best care possible, and I am afraid to say right now that his future is in God's hands. Maybe it's time to start praying."

Maria looked at Sean not in disbelief but more in sorrow, saying, "I have not prayed for years, and I feel somewhat hypocritical to begin now asking God to save my husband's life."

Sean replied, "God never stops listening. He will listen to whatever you have to say to Him."

It was 9:30 PM when Sean decided to leave the hospital since Dan's condition had not changed over the past several hours. As Sean began his drive home, he called Sister Jeannie, with whom he had become friends since the bike-building exercise , to give her an update on Maria and Dan. Sean said with great sorrow to Sister Jeannie, "I just wish Maria had some other family or friends that could be with her right now. Going through such a life-changing event is hard, but it is even harder when you go through it alone."

Before Sister Jeannie responded, she thought how that last comment from Sean must have come as a result of him going through the loss of Kate basically alone, but she decided now was not the time to ask. Before they hung up, Sister Jeannie added, "Let me see what I can do about trying to find someone who can be with Maria right now." Sister Jeannie did not share with Sean what she had up her sleeve because she knew it might be a long shot.

21

Plan B

SLEEP DID NOT come easy for Sean during the night. Thoughts of Maria and Dan as well as of the upcoming board meeting on Friday raced through his head. Back and forth his mind went over one issue and then another. It seemed like just when he was starting to get into some deep thought concerning next steps of one issue, then the other major issue would crowd out that thinking. Sean laid in bed all night, trying to work everything out in his mind only to have it remain a spotty mess. By the time daylight started to peek through the cracks in his blinds, Sean had finally fallen asleep. Unfortunately, the alarm clock woke him just thirty minutes later.

He had a 7 AM meeting with Pat Scott this morning so they could strategize about the board meeting on Friday. This would also allow Sean to refocus on the problems at hand involving Mike Polaski, the future of the Futures Academy, and finally his ability to remain employed. Sean did not at all regret the time he spent the day before helping Maria and Dan, but it had been time he had originally planned to use in preparation for the upcoming board meeting and he would now have to scramble a bit to catch up.

As Sean pulled into the Health System parking lot at 6:50 AM, he recognized Pat Scott's car, a white 2012 Volvo S 80, which made him smile since the car matched Pat in terms of having a reputation of being both reliable and safe. Sean knew he felt "safe" around Pat since he could be open and honest with her; she was also very reliable, as well as being available whenever he needed her assistance and counsel.

The meeting began promptly in Pat's office, and she jumped right in by stating, "I've got some bad news. The board meeting has been moved up to Thursday morning. It will be held here in the System Office boardroom." Sean felt like he had just been punched in the gut, realizing that he and Pat now had even less time to prepare than originally expected.

Sean finally recovered and asked, "How come it was moved up a day?" Pat had learned late last night from the Board Chair, Sister Elizabeth, that Charles Brown had changed his travel plans and would be back in town tomorrow night. Since Brown was the reason why the board meeting was originally scheduled for Friday, Sister Elizabeth and other Board members felt it was better to have the meeting sooner rather than later given that Brown would be in town.

Sean added quite quickly, "That may be good for the Board, but it gives us less time to prepare our defense."

"Not ideal, I know, but this is what we've got to deal with," Pat replied.

Pat went on to share how she had been in active discussions with many of the Board members, and at present it appeared the Board was split 50/50 on the question of the Futures Academy. There were eight members in favor of it continuing, and eight against. Those against were being led by Brown, who was also positioning the argument that if the Futures Academy was disbanded, then Sean as the leader of this effort should also be fired. This point did not get a response from Sean, but, inside, his stomach was churning with angst. He then did the quick math in his head and asked, "If there are seventeen Board members, who is unaccounted for?"

Pat smiled and said, "Guess."

Sean thought for a moment while running through the Board members' names and then said, "Let me think. The one member who has not decided which way to vote yet is…Sam Porter."

Pat responded, "Give the man a lucky cigar for guessing the right answer."

Sean's facial expression changed as soon as Pat confirmed that the lone holdout was indeed Sam Porter. He blurted, "We are screwed if all of our hopes and plans depend upon the vote of Sam Porter."

This caught Pat by somewhat of a surprise, and she asked why this would be the case. Sean went on to explain that years ago, Sam Porter's firm had a contract with Divine Mercy to provide billing services for employed physicians and homecare services. During a routine audit, it was learned that Sam's firm was overbilling the patients and their insurance companies for homecare services, resulting in higher payments to the hospital. To make things worse, Sam's firm was pocketing the difference between what was paid and what should have been paid.

Sean explained, "We quietly worked with all of the insurance companies to correct the overbilling problems and paid whatever fines were levied. In return, they agreed to keep this out of the press. As for Sam Porter's firm's contract, it was terminated for cause, and needless to say he was not happy. Sam was also required to reimburse the hospital for all of the fines and penalties associated with this investigation. Sam went to Charles Brown to try to get this decision reversed through political channels but to no avail.

Porter finally agreed to pay the hospital the amount due only when I threatened to go public with what he and his firm had done. A few years later, Porter worked with Brown to get the additional $22 million in funding from the State to compensate for the increase in care provided to the poor and uninsured. As a payback for the Health System getting the additional funds, Greene was successful in getting Porter elected to the Board. And as part of this process, Brown got another supporter of his on the Board. It seems like ever since then, Porter and Brown have become closer."

Pat then asked, "If Porter and Brown are so close, then why is Porter holding out on announcing his vote until the board meeting?"

Sean thought for moment and then added, "Typical Chicago politics, but for whatever the reason, it will be sure to benefit Porter and not us. In my opinion, we might as well count his vote as one against us, which means it does not look good for us or the Futures program."

* * *

As Sean and Pat's meeting ended, Pat noticed an email from her sister Sue asking Pat to call her ASAP. When Pat heard Sue's voice, she started by saying, "Things are getting desperate here. The board meeting has been moved up from Friday to Thursday morning. Please tell me some good news."

Sue went on to explain in a very straightforward, no-nonsense voice, "I have some good news and also some bad news. Which would you like to hear first?"

Pat sighed and said, "I could use some good news today."

So Sue went on to explain, "The good news is our agents have found some significant concerns involving Brown and his union activities in other states. Apparently, Brown has been traveling out of state to expand the presence of the union, and he has been using his old intimidation tactics quite success-fully. In one situation, we have found evidence that Brown ordered destruc-tion of two trucks owned by a firm that was unwilling to support the union. The best part is that on Monday of this week, we were able to capture many of these threats as a result of wire taps, and it is clear Brown had no knowl-edge of such efforts given how he was bragging about what would happen if the companies did not comply with his wishes. I have discussed this with my supervisors, and we feel we have enough to seek a warrant for his arrest."

Pat was excited to get some good news, and she offered, "So if that is the good news, then what is the bad news?"

Sue went on to explain, "We feel that given Brown's connections within the state of Illinois, we cannot attempt to secure an arrest warrant in your State. Our fear is that if Brown finds out about a pending arrest warrant, he will either try to flee the State or get his lawyers involved, ruining the element of surprise. The more we can keep this secret up until the arrest, the better."

Pat added, "Based on what I have learned about Brown, I would say your concern is valid and we do not want to miss this chance to nail the bastard by word getting out prematurely."

Sue replied, "The only way to pull this off, given your new timeframe, is to quickly find a judge in another state to review and sign the arrest warrant. However, this process normally takes weeks."

Pat digested all that she just heard and said, "There has to be something you can do before Thursday. What can be done since we are so close?'

Sue added, "We are trying to present all of our evidence to a federal judge in Cleveland who has experience with this type of case."

Pat sounded a little impatient when she closed with, "I don't care what you have to do—just get this done by Thursday morning."

After Sue hung up her cell phone, she had to chuckle with how that call just ended with Pat going all "boss like" on her, giving Sue direction for things over which Pat had no control over. "Oh well," Sue thought, "once a big sister, always a big sister."

* * *

Sean arrived on the Neuro ICU floor and expected to find Maria and Dan's parents in the room but instead found only a nurse taking care of Dan. Sean then learned that Maria and Dan's parents where in the conference room with Dr. Duncan. Sean walked down to the conference room and paused before he went in, saying a short prayer for all those in the room who were having what he believed was one of the most difficult conversations between a health care provider and a family member.

As Sean entered the room, he could tell Dr. Duncan had already broached the subject of Dan's prognosis and also organ donation. The tears were flowing and the tissue box was being passed around the table. As Sean sat down, Dr. Duncan added that in the State of Illinois, the spouse has the legal right to make the organ donation decision. This last piece of the complicated puzzle really caught both Maria and Dan's parents by surprise. It seemed like they all assumed the responsibility for the hard decision would fall to Dan's parents. This new information just stunned Maria and appeared to anger Dan's parents. Dan's parents were very religious, and they were still trying to digest all that had happened since yesterday morning when they got the call from Maria informing them of their son's accident. They obviously had not slept well last night, and the stress of the situation was really beginning to show.

Dan's mother spoke first, saying, "I believe it is in God's hands and no one should be making that decision except God."

Dan's Dad had been sitting quietly and then erupted, "Maria has treated our son like dirt for the three years they dated and now the almost two years they have been married. It just does not seem right for someone who has treated our son so poorly to have the ultimate responsibility for this decision."

Up until now, Maria had tried to be on her best behavior with Dan's parents, but upon hearing his father's comments, she lost it: "How dare you say those things about my relationship with your son? I love him and he loves me, and if you cared about us, why didn't you return all of our phone calls?"

Dan's father replied, "I did not return those calls because I did not want to talk with you."

That last comment cut very deep, and finally Sean had to step in and say, "We are here to discuss Dan's care and potential plans if things do not work out like we hope. Please—let's get back to the question raised by Dr. Duncan."

There was complete silence immediately after Sean spoke, and finally Dr. Duncan ended the conversation by saying they would continue to monitor Dan's condition and then sit down again at the end of the day to discuss next steps.

As Maria and Dr. Duncan left the room, Sean stayed behind and introduced himself to Dan's parents. Sean was quite impressed with both Dan's mother and father and could only imagine the pain they were going through. Sean offered whatever assistance he could provide to them while they were in town. Sean also shared that he was not aware of the history between Maria and themselves, but he did say he had begun to notice a positive change in Maria lately.

Dan's father interjected, "We did not want Dan to marry Maria because of the way she was treating him. Our Dan is such a good-hearted young man, and we felt he deserved better. He used to say that we didn't see what he saw in Maria—and he was right. If there is a good bone in her body, I never saw it."

After a long pause, Dan's mother said, "He also used to remind us that people can change, honey. And I have to admit that Dan shared a few things with me this past weekend that show she might have started to change for the better. For one thing, she actually spoke to me on the phone when I called. And then Dan said she had started being more understanding of others since joining that work group." Sean did not explain his role with the Futures Academy, but he was glad to hear that their son had begun to notice a positive change in Maria.

Sean took a risk and asked both parents to try to also help Maria during this difficult period. Sean could see some positive reaction to what he just said from Dan's mother, but Dan's father said quite coldly, "Our first responsibility is to our son and not that witch he married."

As Sean and Dan's parents left the conference room, Sean walked into the

Nurse Manager's office and closed the door. He needed a second to regroup before he went into Dan's room when his cell phone rang. It was Sister Jeannie asking for an update on how Dan was doing. Sean provided the update on Dan's condition and also some information related to the meeting with Dr. Duncan and then the meeting afterward with Dan's parents. Sister Jeannie asked more about the meeting with Dan's parents, and Sean responded that it did not go well and they were going to need a Plan B in order to help both Dan and Maria. "Without any support, I am afraid we are going to lose both Dan and Maria for good." Before he completed their call, Sean added, "I know from our last call that you were working on something. Please do whatever it takes to get help for Maria."

22

PAYBACKS ARE A "BITCH"

A S SEAN WAS getting into his car, his cell phone rang and he couldn't help but think, "What next?"

It was Pat Scott. "Are you ready for the board meeting?" she asked.

"I'm as ready as I am ever going to be," he answered.

Pat laughed good naturedly at Sean's response. She knew she and Sean were going into a battle today with some members of the Board, and she was glad Sean was on her side. Sean too was glad to have Pat in his corner.

"I spoke to Sam Porter late last night," Pat explained. "And he maintains that he still has not made up his mind about which way he is going to vote today."

Sean let out a questioning sort of grunt that said, "I'll believe it when I see it."

"He and Brown had a recent falling out," Pat continued, "and Porter says he is still trying to keep an open mind regarding the Futures Academy and your employment." Porter had also shared with Pat how Brown had been trying to get his vote over the past few days by calling multiple times while

203

Brown was out of town. Porter stated that he was rather traditional and liked to conduct his work face to face and not over the phone.

"Pat," Sean asked. "What do you think could happen today at the board meeting that could help our chances of success? Is there any chance of hope?"

"Well," Pat said with a touch of uncertainty in her voice, "I'm working on something that may or may not come together before the meeting. My hope is that if everything comes together, Brown may get a taste of his own medicine."

This last statement caught Sean's attention because he had learned since working with Pat that she never seemed to divulge anything unless there was a high chance of success. He only hoped that whatever she was working on would come through because he had very little other than the success story of the Futures Academy to help sway the Board's vote. Although many of the group members had been on a positive growth path, none had yet been promoted, leaving Sean without much tangible evidence of success.

"Pat, it seems like you have grown to dislike Brown as much as I do," Sean said. Pat's only response was something she had shared a while back: "No one likes a bully."

* * *

Pat was sitting at her desk with her head in her hands when her cell phone rang. It was twenty minutes until the board meeting would begin, and she was allowing herself a few minutes to wallow in worry. She'd put on her game face soon, but in this moment, all she could think about was how badly she wanted to help turn the hospital system around and how much of a failure she'd feel like if she didn't succeed. Her eyes were closed as she rubbed her forehead nervously until her phone rang. She could see by the caller ID that it was her sister, Sue.

"We were able to get a federal judge in Cleveland to sign Brown's arrest warrant this morning," Sue said.

Pat silently made the sign of the cross and said, "Thank you Jesus."

"The FBI agents are at the airport on a jet waiting to take off for the flight into Chicago," Sue continued with a sound of reservation in her voice.

Pat knew that it would be a short flight and that the airport was only ten minutes from the Health System offices. "Does this mean your agents might make it before our meeting is over?" she asked.

Sue answered by saying, "Pat, it's storming in Cleveland right now. The plane is on a ground hold."

"Of course," Pat said. "So close and yet so far."

"Look, we have our best field agent, Ed Carter handling this case, and I can assure you he will do everything in his power to be there on time. As soon as the storm passes, they can take off. Let's just hold our breath—or maybe you can have one of the nuns say a prayer—and I will call you when I know more."

Pat then replied, "If we miss this chance today, Sue, we might never get a chance to nail this bastard—and the damage to this Health System and some talented executives will be done."

* * *

As Sean was standing in the hallway outside of the Boardroom, he looked out at the beautiful skyline of downtown Chicago and thought how difficult a time Dan, Maria, and Dan's parents were going through on such a beautiful day. Somehow his challenges did not even come close to what they were experiencing at this moment in time.

Sean entered the boardroom and took a seat next to Pat. The meeting was due to begin shortly and neither Brown nor Porter were there. Sean wondered, "Was it a coincidence or was there more to their joint absence?"

Sean leaned over to Pat and said, "I have two updates and one question. The first update is that I got a call this morning from Dr. Goldberg and learned Maria's husband's condition is starting to deteriorate. The second is I just learned from the head of our security that Sam Porter was spotted with Charles Brown this morning having breakfast." Sean could see both updates were registering with Pat when she asked, "So what was your question?" Sean continued by asking, "So after this meeting, will we have the thrill of victory or the agony of defeat?"

Pat responded, "Not sure since I believe this could go either way." What Sean did not share with Pat was how both Dr. Goldberg and Luther Jackson, Head of Security, knew about this important board meeting and how they both basically said the same thing: "Don't take any crap from anybody today." Sean continued to be amazed about who knew what about what was going on and also about how some people really cared about him as well as the future of the organization.

Sean had just opened his notes to look at them one more time when the door swung open and Brown entered, followed by Porter. By the way they were both smiling, Sean had a sinking feeling that Brown had cut some type of deal while out for breakfast this morning. That thought jived with what Pat had shared the other day about how Porter was traditional and liked doing business face to face.

Even before Brown and Porter were seated, Sister Elizabeth, the Health System Board Chair who was somewhat perturbed that Brown had to make a grand entrance, called the meeting to order and started with a prayer. She then turned the meeting over to Pat Scott.

Pat began with a very strong and commanding voice: "This special board meeting was called to discuss two items: first, to review the Mike Polaski incident and, second, to decide on the fate of the Futures Academy.

Brown interrupted by saying, "There is also the matter of what should be done with the future of Sean O'Brien."

Just hearing the tone in Brown's voice upset Sean, but he concealed his anger quite well. He remembered the story of the duck that looks so peaceful on the surface of the lake while paddling like hell underneath. If he were to have any chance of success in this meeting, he'd have to do the same.

"Sean, I'd now like to turn the meeting over to you," Pat said with a look of warmth and encouragement.

Brown shifted in his seat and exhaled audibly, irritated with the familiarity Pat seemed to be showing to Sean.

Sean began by reviewing the Mike Polaski incident. It was the elephant in the room and there was no escaping it; his hope was to get it out of the way first and then end on a high note by talking about the positive success of the Futures Academy.

Before he could get to the features and benefits of the program, however, Porter blurted, "I find it hard to believe that someone in charge of this group of young executives would have no knowledge of Mr. Polaski's illegal activities."

Sean responded with a short answer. "No, I was not aware of any of the problems involving Mike Polaski. In fact, I will tell you what I told others. Mike Polaski screwed up, but he is not a screw-up. He made a terrible mistake, one for which he will pay for the rest of his young life."

"It may be true that it was a mistake," Porter replied, "and even that Mr. Polaski is not a bad person. But the fact still remains that he conducted these illegal activities while under *your mentorship*. How out of touch does that make you?"

Sean said, "Like any good leader, it makes me feel very uncomfortable that this happened and that none of us knew anything about it."

In addition to Porter's question, there were others from the group, and Sean could tell from these questions that there was a great deal of misinformation out there concerning the entire matter. Brown kept making comments too that seemed to add confusion as to what had really happened.

Sean worked hard to keep his composure and answered one question at a time as calmly as he could.

At the first chance he got, he deftly transitioned the conversation into the feature and benefits of the Futures Academy. He knew the Board had heard some of the information, but he wanted to make sure that they heard every important detail. Sean could tell by just reading the body language of many in the room that they were not aware of some of the information he was now sharing. In fact, several members began to take notes. The numbers related to the cost associated with CEO turnover seemed to blow most of the Board members away. Sean highlighted that the estimated cost of one CEO departure was $5.6 million and that given this understanding that there could be as many as eight CEO departures in the near future, the *total* cost of CEO turnover could be a whopping $44.8 million. That last figure seemed to just hang in the air.

About fifteen minutes into the discussion, Charles Brown announced, "Okay, I think we have enough information to call for a vote." Before Sean could respond, both Pat and Sister Elizabeth said at the same time, "Sean, continue with your presentation." Sister Elizabeth was irritated over Brown being late and found this latest interruption to be just one more irritation. Pat was also stalling for time in hopes that the FBI agents would arrive before the meeting's close.

Sean continued for another forty-five minutes, and then answered many questions. He was surprised by the number and extent of the questions, and he was happy to answer each question in full detail. Finally, there was stillness to the meeting that became somewhat uncomfortable, and then Sam Porter asked, "Are you here to tell me that with all of the problems associated with Mike Polaski that you had no knowledge of his taking bribes from outside vendors?"

Porter just couldn't let the Polaski incident go. Sean repeated his earlier answer: "Like any good leader, it makes me feel very uncomfortable that this happened and that none of us knew anything about it."

By now it was 11:20 AM and Sean knew he could not delay the vote any longer. Sister Elizabeth seemed to agree. "Being there are no further questions," she said, "all those in favor of continuing with the Holy Spirit Health System Futures Academy, say 'I.'"

As Sister Elizabeth counted the votes, she announced that it was tied with eight for and eight against. "We still need your vote, Mr. Porter," Sister Elizabeth said.

Porter smiled and said, "Nay."

Brown then stepped in and called for a second vote. "All those in favor of Sean O'Brien's employment being immediately terminated say 'I.'" Again, the votes were eight for and eight against, with Sam Porter trailing at the end. He gave his vote and it was…against Sean. The silence in the room was deafening while Brown stood up and said he and Porter had a meeting to attend. With that the meeting was adjourned, and those who had voted in support of the Futures Academy remained behind while those who had voted to terminate the program and Sean's employment left quite hastily.

Pat, Sister Elizabeth, and Sean were gathered by the boardroom window and began to discuss what had just occurred when Sister Elizabeth said to Sean, "I am so sorry for what just happened. I was praying so hard for a different outcome."

Sean was still processing what had just occurred and said, "Don't worry about me. Worry about the other twelve individuals who are still part of the Futures Academy and for the future of the Holy Spirit Health System."

Just as Pat was about to tell Sister Elizabeth and Sean of her plan on how to deal with Charles Brown, Sean asked while looking out the window, "What are all those press trucks dong outside the main entrance of our building?" At the same time, Pat received a text message from her sister, stating, "Agents should be there in less than 10 minutes."

Before Pat could say anything, Sean had already left the boardroom and was taking the steps three floors down to get outside as quickly as possible. As Sean came through the main entrance doors, he could see Brown positioned in front of the reporters and cameramen. Brown waited until all of the TV cameras were in place and the radio stations had their microphones in position to hear what he had to say. Sean noticed that there were also some members of the local community present, and then he figured that Brown had this all orchestrated. Brown wanted nothing more than to be like a king presenting some important news and to have loyal fans there to show their support.

What Sean could not understand was why Lilly Black, the very supportive community organizer and advocate for Divine Mercy Hospital and speaker at his going away party, was present. He did not have much time to think about Lilly when he heard Brown's bellowing voice. "As many of you know, the Divine Mercy Hospital System has recently suffered from a recent major blow by way of the corrupt dealings of one of its hospital executives, Mike Polaski. We have worked tirelessly to root out this corruption and set the hospital on a new path. The system's Board has just finished meeting, and it has been decided that the best course of action is to immediately shut down the Leadership Development program under which Mr. Polaski was mentored— called the Futures Academy—as well as to terminate the employment of the leader of this program, Sean O'Brien."

Sean thought how predictable it was that Brown would step in to take credit for the recent terminations when Brown continued, "As many of my constituents know, I am a real advocate for the less fortunate and I am against any form of corporate corruption..."

Brown was just getting ready to launch into one of his now famous rants when three handsomely dressed men approached him and interrupted. The one man identified himself as Agent Ed Carter, FBI. Carter continued by asking, "Are you Charles Brown?" to which Brown responded in the affirmative. Carter, a stocky agent who had graying hair and a well-trimmed, fit body continued by speaking very loudly so everyone could hear: "Charles Brown, you are under arrest for racketeering under the RICO statutes, accepting bribes to influence union contracts and also for the destruction of property in the states of Illinois, Ohio, and Pennsylvania." It was at that moment that Sean noticed the bandages on Brown's left hand, and he later learned that the FBI had actually caught Brown on tape firebombing trucking equipment at one of the nonunion companies he was trying to intimidate into joining his union.

Brown was so shocked at what was happening that it took a moment to regroup and say, "Let me see that warrant. This is bogus—just another example of the government trying to keep the less fortunate down." Agent Carter handed Brown a copy of the warrant as Brown was trying to read the charges and see what Judge in the state of Illinois had the guts to sign a warrant against him. As Brown was deciphering the signature, Agent Carter spoke again: "This warrant was signed by the honorable Alan Krigstein out of the third district in Cleveland, Ohio." Agent Carter could tell the name of Judge Krigstein seemed to strike a chord in Brown's long term-memory when he then got really close to Brown's ear so the microphones would not pick up what he was about to say: "Here is a personal message for you from Judge Krigstein: 'Paybacks are a bitch.'" It was at that moment that Brown remembered that Krigstein was the one he had beaten up in high school for not allowing Brown to cheat off of him during a final exam. "Someday Brown will get what is coming to him," Alan's dad had said back then. Alan was nothing but happy to sign the arrest warrant to fulfill a promise his Dad made almost forty years ago.

The two other FBI agents proceeded to handcuff Brown and take him to the waiting car. Agent Carter, who was experienced with handling high-profile cases involving the press, stepped in front of the microphones and provided some additional information so the press would have the full story for their noontime newscast. The one thing that struck Sean as somewhat odd was when Agent Carter mentioned how a case of this magnitude would never be possible without the cooperation of so many members of the community. He continued by saying, "This is a wonderful example of how when law enforcement and the community work together, great things can happen."

As the press conference wrapped up, Sean suddenly realized that Lilly Black, his old Divine Mercy friend, was standing next to him. "No one messes with my adopted son," she said, protectively referring to Sean.

"How'd you know about the press conference?" Sean asked. Lilly shared how her nephew worked at one of the TV stations and she got a call saying that something big was going to happen at the Health System office. "Since I knew about you and this board meeting, I just had to be here to learn what happened. We all did," she finished, motioning toward the faces of several people who knew and respected Sean. He looked around, slowly trying to absorb all the faces and feeling overwhelmed with appreciation for Lilly and his other supporters in the community.

23

JUST GET IT DONE

SEAN WAS HAPPY that he was able to get out of town for the weekend to decompress. Sean and Kate had a small cabin on a lake about two hours outside the city which was used a great deal when the children were younger. Since Kate died, Sean had been there only a handful of times, mainly to check on the condition of the cabin. Sean knew he could go to the Lake cabin and try to relax and think through all that had just happened. He was tense and tired from the events of the past week and he needed to get away.

One of the best parts of visiting the cabin was sitting lakeside during sunsets. As the sun went down, the wind often stopped, which made the lake appear like glass. The reflection of the sun off the lake was just mesmerizing and for Sean filled with many fond memories. Sean also loved this place because it always afforded him the opportunity to focus on his three favorite things when dealing with strife in his life: place, prayer, and person. This was definitely a special place where he could often pray and connect with God. But this time was different since he did not have his Kate with him to talk to about whatever was troubling him.

At 1:45 PM on Saturday, Sean decided to call Maria and see how everything was going. Sean asked about how Maria was doing, and she paused and finally said, "I'm afraid I am going to lose my best friend." Sean listened intently. He knew from experience there was a process someone goes through when they are about to lose a loved one, and he thought how Maria was at least moving out of the denial and anger phases, which was good given the severity of Dan's injuries.

"Sean, Dr. Duncan said that Dan's organs are working overtime to support his injured body and they might weaken. I think he is truly on the downward slope."

"Maria, we don't know what is going to happen to Dan, but I can tell you this. There are many people praying for him—including those from the Futures Academy—and you are not, and never will be, alone."

Sean could hear Maria sobbing quietly on the other end of the phone. Finally, she sniffled, cleared her throat, and said, "Speaking of the Futures Academy, what is going to happen to us Future folks now that Mike went to jail and Brown got served on TV?"

Maria had learned about Brown's dramatic departure, by speaking with the nurses on the unit. Once word broke, everyone turned on their TVs, including in the patient lounge, to watch the televised events unfold. Maria chuckled and said how the look on Brown's face was priceless, but it was also interesting how Sam Porter was standing quite proudly behind Brown before the FBI arrived, basking in the glow of this opportunity. Once Agent Carter began to read Brown the arrest warrant, you could see Porter gradually slide out of the picture like he wanted to get as far away as possible from what was occurring. Maria added in regard to Porter's exodus from the press conference, "It was like watching a rat trying to get off a sinking ship." Sean loved to hear some animation in Maria's voice as she told him about the press conference and he had to admit too that the rat bit was a great analogy.

"But what next for the Futures Academy?" Maria asked.

Sean gave Maria a high level overview just like he had done for the Futures Group by conference call shortly after the board meeting. "The Board voted to terminate the Futures Academy," Sean said "as well as me." He also added given Charles Brown's arrest that he was unsure of what if anything the Board would do differently than originally stated at the meeting. Sean did share that Pat Scott had agreed *not* to send any internal announcements about how the Board voted until early next week.

"They fired you?" Maria asked indignantly. Sean was surprised that Maria seemed most concerned about him as he had expected her to focus more on the fate of the Futures group. "Unbelievable," she said, "You are one of the first real leaders that has stood up at that organization and they want to let you go. I have learned more being mentored by you in eleven months than I did in all of the years under the leadership of Tina Blake."

The call ended with Maria agreeing to keep Sean posted on Dan's condition and Sean offered that if anything changed with the Futures Academy, he would keep her updated. Sean also shared that he was out of town for the weekend but he would return if anything changed with Dan's condition.

* * *

The only real "work" Sean did over the rest of the weekend was to take a call from Sister Jeannie early on Sunday morning, before church service. Sister Jeannie gave Sean an update on her efforts to help Maria, but shared that money might be a problem. Sean went into his old CEO mode and barked, "I do not care what the costs, just get it done." Sean proceeded to give Sister Jeannie his credit card number and told her to charge whatever she needed to his account. After he hung up, he laughed that he just gave someone free use of his personal credit card; if it was anyone other than Sister Jeannie, they might be out taking their "bucket list" trip at his expense.

Fortunately, he did not have to worry about that with Sister Jeannie since she had taken a vow of poverty.

The last thing Sister Jeannie said was, "I will move Heaven and earth to get this done. I will not let you down." Given the rather chilly relationship Sister Jeannie and Sean had had over the years, Sean was happy to see how they were both working together to help out someone in need.

24

NEVER WASTE A GOOD CRISIS

PRIOR TO ARRIVING at the Health System office on Monday morning, Sean had stopped in at the hospital to check in on Dan and learned that not much had changed over the weekend. Maria was still sleeping so Sean had a chance to say a quick hello to Dan's parents. Dan's mom, Beth, was sitting at the bedside holding her son's hand while Sean spoke to his father, Keith. Keith said that the CEO from the Gift of Life organization had been in over the weekend. The Gift of Life CEO Howard Nathan explained how the organ donation process worked and also shared that as many as eight major organs might be used to help other patients on the organ donation waiting lists. Keith said, "We all are beginning to realize that Dan may not make it and that we may have some tough decisions to make soon." Sean mentioned that he would stop back later, and as he was leaving, Keith said, "Thank you for all you are doing for our son and his wife. We understand you used to be the CEO of this hospital, and I just want you to know everyone has been so kind and offering to help in any way possible.

In fact, the one night nurse offered to take some of our laundry home and will bring it back tonight."

Sean was happy to hear that the focus on treating every patient as if they were a member of the family was still part of the culture he had worked so hard to build.

* * *

Sean arrived at the Health System office just in time to meet with Pat at her office for their early meeting before he met with the Futures Academy. He could not help but notice that this morning there were more cars in the parking lot than usual at this hour, including those of Steve Driver and Tina Blake. Maybe Pat was starting to have a positive impact on these two characters.

Pat began the meeting by filling Sean in on what she had been doing behind the scenes with the FBI and her sister to help advance the investigation into Charles Brown. Sean was both shocked and impressed at Pat's tenacity with pursuing Brown. In fact, at one point, Pat used the word "bastard" when referring to Brown, which indicated some of the emotion that was driving her to bring Brown down. The more he learned about Pat, the more Sean liked her. It would be sad when her interim role with Holy Spirit Health System ended.

Pat then shared about the many discussions she had had with the Board over the weekend. The bottom line was that Sean was very happy with the five decisions the Board had made over the weekend and they both agreed Sean would share these outcomes with the Futures Group later in the day. Pat smiled and asked, "What do you think?"

"Well," Sean said, "that explains why I saw both Driver and Blake's cars in the parking lot this morning."

Sean then began to smile, and said, "You and the Board have been very busy over the weekend." Sean then asked about what prompted the additional decisions outside of the Futures Academy, and Pat responded, "I can't work with people I cannot trust. Second, I learned long ago that every crisis is an opportunity, and I decided not to waste a good crisis to get something done sooner than would have otherwise taken much longer to accomplish."

Sean processed what Pat had just shared and said to himself, "Learn something new every day."

25

WE ARE ALL HUMAN

SEAN WALKED INTO the morning meeting with the Futures Academy just behind Jim Piper and Rachel Pepper, a few minutes late because he had taken a last minute call from Maryanne Richmond. Maryanne wanted to share some good news with Sean about how the hospital finances and quality results had dramatically improved. Sean must have seemed a little inpatient with trying to hurry Maryanne along so he would not be late for his meeting, when she added, "The real reason why I am calling is to say thank you for whatever role you had in the sudden and pleasurable fall of Charles Brown. Having that man out of my hair will make my life so much better."

Sean congratulated Maryanne and her team for posting such positive results and reminded her, "We as executives only stay in these jobs as long as we post the results needed to help the organization survive and thrive. And regarding Brown, all I can say is the next time you see Pat Scott, you owe that woman a big hug." Maryanne knew Sean at times liked to speak in code, and she inferred from this comment that it was Pat who had played a bigger role in the demise of Charles Brown.

The meeting began with a prayer that was said by Harry Klein, although Sean became a bit distracted when a new text message arrived for him from Sister Jeannie, who was sitting across the room from him.

"The package will be delivered later this morning," the text said. Sean was glad to get this message, but he also wondered why Sister Jeannie was texting during the prayer. "Wasn't that some church violation?" he wondered, while smiling to himself. Maybe God made exceptions for important circumstances such as these.

As Sean looked around the room, he could not help but notice that two of the Futures Academy members were not there, Mike Polaski and Maria Smith. Obviously, they were absent for different reasons, but they were both alike missing from this group of talented leaders that Sean had grown to love and respect.

After everyone was seated, the first order of business was for Sean to check in to hear what rumors were swirling since last Thursday. It seemed like most of the rumors were pretty accurate except for the one where Pat Scott was also being let go.

Kylene Knight asked, "Did anyone else see the announcement from Pat Scott about the resignation of Steve Driver effective today?" Some, who had not, quickly picked up their smart phones to check their email and noticed that they had all received the email Kylene had just referenced. People commented about the tone and timing of the announcement and how Pat Scott was not pulling any punches as to why Steve Driver was leaving the organization. In fact, Kylene read the one sentence that was highly unusual for similar announcements that had occurred in the past: "Steve no longer fits in with the future direction of the Holy Spirit Health System." Kylene continued to read on to the last part of this announcement, which said, "There will be other announcements later this week about additional leadership changes," to which all eyes turned to Sean to explain what that last line meant.

Before Sean could speak, Sister Jeannie added that she and her entire congregation supported the decision announced in the memo and any of the other announcements that would be made later this week. There was a short pause that gave Sean a chance to digest Sister Jeannie's comment, and the only realistic explanation was that Pat Scott had gotten to the key Religious Leadership late last night to get their support for what was going to occur this week. Over the years, Sean had learned the value of having the good Sisters behind major decisions because most of the employees and others would turn to them for counsel and support. It was obvious Pat Scott had learned the same lesson and was doing her homework in advance of what was going to happen this week in terms of personnel changes.

Sean then said, "Where would you like me to begin?"

Blake Jones, CEO of St. James Community Hospital, said, "Why don't you start at the part where the Futures Academy is being discontinued? I heard the Board voted to terminate our Futures Academy, and I can't say that I can fault their decision. We have been together for almost a year and so far no one has been promoted from this group into a Senior Executive position. What's more, one of our 'all-star' members has been arrested for taking bribes, and let's be honest—another of our members has such a poor demeanor that she would need a personality makeover to ever change." Everyone knew the last person Blake had just referenced was Maria Smith.

Finally, Sister Jeannie said in anger, "Can't you show a little mercy for Maria given what she is going through?"

Blake replied that he was sorry if he was being insensitive to Maria, but he was just trying to make a point that from a Board member's perspective, he could understand why they would vote to terminate the program.

Finally, Sean decided to end Blake's rant before he embarrassed himself anymore. Seizing this "teachable moment," Sean walked over to the white board and drew two lines that intersected in the middle, similar to the lines of a horizontal x and vertical y axis that they all had learned about in high school geometry class. Sean went on to explain, "What you see here are two intersection lines that represent our careers." The intersecting horizontal and vertical lines divided the page into four quadrants. Sean pointed to the top right quadrant and said, "This section represents those who start out on the right path and just keep on going up with promotion after promotion. The top left section represents those who start out strong and then "self-destruct" by doing something stupid. The bottom left section represents those that start out bad and just keep getting worse. The last section, those in the bottom left quadrant, start out bad and for some reason are able to turn things around and eventually be successful."

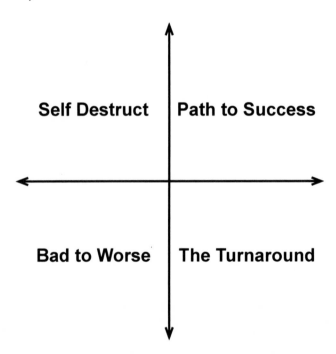

Self Destruct   **Path to Success**

Bad to Worse   **The Turnaround**

"Ladies and gentlemen, we stand at the intersection of these lines everyday of our lives and make decisions as to what direction we are going to go next. Some of us make great decisions and some of us do not. Now, let me ask, who can name leaders who are from outside of our organization and from the Chicago area or our state that seem to fit into each one of these four sections?"

Jim Piper went first, stating, "Since he is from Chicago, I would say President Obama is someone whose name could go in that top right section. He worked hard throughout his career and at a very young age became the first African American President of the United States. Pretty impressive." Many in the group agreed so Sean wrote *President Obama* in that top right section. "Political preferences aside," Sean said, "it seems fair to say that Barack Obama started on a positive career trajectory and has continued to be successful in his career to date."

Cheryl Butler went next and said, "Sticking with someone local and in politics, I would suggest for the top left quadrant former Illinois Governor Rob Blagojevich. His career seemed to be so bright and then he got greedy and self-destructed." Again all the members seemed to agree with the suggestion made by Cheryl.

There was a longer pause than before until Rachel spoke up and said, "I guess a safe bet for the lower left would be someone like Al Capone, the famous Chicago gangster." This suggestion got a few laughs from the group but seemed to fit the definition perfectly. It took a while for the group to come up with a name for the lower left section and finally Tom Flowers spoke up and said, "As many of you know, I am a big sports fan and a local guy that started out really bad and then turned his life around is Jason Avant."

Sister Jeannie replied, "Can you tell me more about this Jason Avant? I'm not a sports person."

Tom welcomed the opportunity to share some of his vast sports knowledge. "Jason Avant is a professional football player who currently plays in the NFL for the Philadelphia Eagles. Jason grew up on the South Side of Chicago and began selling drugs when he was twelve years old and eventually joined a well-known gang called the Gangster Disciples."

Many in the room did not know the story of Jason Avant, and again it was Sister Jeannie who asked, "How did he turn things around?"

Tom went on to explain, "He had a very strong grandmother who saw his potential and never gave up on him. She took him to church and kept praying that he would be safe and turn things around. He eventually found football and the rest, as they say, is history."

Next Sean suggested, "Let's do the same exercise but now only using names of people that work in the Holy Spirit Health System." As often happens when people talk among themselves, the first names mentioned were more along the negative line.

Blake Jones said, "I believe Mike Polaski is someone whose name should go in the top left section. Mike represented someone who started out strong and then self-destructed by taking the bribes. He had success written all over him and then he threw it all away. His career, if not over, will certainly take a long time to recover." There was an impromptu debate about whether Mike's career was over but all seemed to agree with the choice of Mike's name for the upper left quadrant. Sean wrote Mike's name in the top left section.

Next, Rachel Pepper raised her hand, since she was a product of sixteen years of Catholic education, and said, "Charles Brown is someone I believe who started out bad and just kept getting worse the older he got. He certainly has done a great deal of damage to our Health System and I only hope we can recover from it." Sean did not even wait to hear if the group agreed with Rachel's suggestion as he wrote in Charles Brown's name into the lower left quadrant.

Donna Reuss went next. "Even though not part of our group, I would like to suggest Maryanne Richmond as someone for the top right section. She has steadily risen throughout the leadership ranks and is now a CEO of Divine Mercy Hospital and from what I can tell is doing a great job." The rest of the group did not comment either way on Maryanne, but after about a minute others spoke in agreement with Donna's recommendation. Sean was thinking back on the call he had received this morning from Maryanne where she was telling him about the many good things that were going on at the hospital and how he would definitely support adding Maryanne's name to the top right quadrant. As he wrote her name, a big smile came across his face in recognition of all of her hard work and his efforts to develop her natural talents over the years. Just after Sean had finished writing Maryanne's name in the top right quadrant, Cheryl Butler added, "I would not be surprised if Maryanne becomes the CEO of the Holy Spirit Health System sometime in the future."

Sean just thought, "From your lips to God's ears," regarding this prediction.

There was just one more quadrant to go, but there was a real reluctance for anyone to nominate someone. They all knew that someone might get upset because by definition the person had to start out bad and then turn things around.

With Sean standing patiently at the board, Sister Jeannie stood and said, "I know some may not agree, but I think Maria Smith could well be someone for the lower right quadrant." There was a deafening silence that fell over the room after Sister Jeannie made her suggestion.

It was broken by Blake Jones, who jumped in with, "How in the hell does Maria fit the definition as someone who turned things around?"

In the past, Sister Jeannie had a reputation of not liking confrontation, but not this time. "I agree that Maria has a history of being a tough person to get along with, but I have noticed some real positive changes in her during the past six months that lead me to believe she is changing for the better. I have heard that Maria has been leading an effort to refinance the Health System debt, which will save approximately $6 million in interest expenses per year. In doing this, Maria has led a team of financial leaders from each of our hospitals, and many have commented on what a pleasure it was to work with Maria on this project and how most of the meetings were held in the hospitals and *not* at the health system offices." Sister Jeannie could tell that many in the room knew of the refinancing efforts but not Maria's role with pulling it all together. Sean added that Maria had asked him this morning while visiting to make sure all of the paperwork still got to Pat Scott today for signature so as not to miss the refinancing deadline.

Jim Piper jumped in, "I know I have gotten a great deal of credit for leading the system-wide effort to reduce our healthcare benefit costs by reducing the number of plans from seventeen to three. But I am here to tell you that I could have never done this without Maria's help. She helped me think through how to design the new benefit plans and also how to effectively negotiate our new rates with the remaining health insurance plans. This effort will not only result in the System offering better health insurance benefits to our employees but will also save us $6.5 million per year." Again, Sean could tell that others were not aware of the work Maria had been doing with Jim and his team.

Jim spoke again, saying, "And I might add that she has been a real delight to work with throughout this entire process. She allowed me to take the lead and helped wherever and whenever I asked for it. She can still be a tough businesswoman, but she seems to be tempering that with a bit more congeniality."

As Sean was standing there, he was thinking how two members of this group played major roles in saving the Health System money while their bosses, Driver and Blake, just took a back seat on both efforts. "Who said this group was not making an impact on the future of the Health System?" he asked.

As Sean looked around the room, there seemed to be agreement with Maria's name being added to the bottom right quadrant so he wrote it down.

As Sean was writing Maria's name, he heard Donna Reuss ask, "Sean, how did you come up with this concept?"

Sean shared, "I got the idea for this visual after watching the hit movie 'Castaway' starring Tom Hanks. As you may remember, at the end of the movie, Tom Hanks' character is standing at the intersection of four country roads, trying to decide which direction he wants to go for the next part of his life. He had survived a terrible plane crash, lived alone on an island for many years, was rescued at sea, and then came home to a hero's welcome to learn his fiancée had married someone else. In spite of all those challenges, he was given a second chance at life. The image of him standing at the intersection of those four country roads struck me because we stand at an 'intersection' everyday, making decisions that will affect our careers."

"Everybody whose name is on the Board in one of those four quadrants is just like you and I, who will make decisions that will impact our respective careers. I want you to be aware of this because as we have seen, for those heading in the right direction, there is great promise and success that awaits. For those that slip up, there is great angst and penalty associated with each wrong turn. Just look at what has happened to both Mike Polaski and Charles Brown. That being said, all those who have screwed up are human beings. We all make mistakes and deserve a second chance."

At that point Blake stood up and said, "I get the four sections and the control we have to have over our careers. I get that we are responsible for what happens in our lives and our careers. But I cannot agree with what you said about forgiveness since Mike and Maria's problems are self-inflicted and they should pay heavily for their mistakes! People that screw up that badly do not deserve a second chance, and their careers should take a serious hit or be over with."

Sean, along with everybody in the room, was shocked by the intensity with which Blake spoke—so much so that Sean was afraid he was going to lose the group and the messages he had hoped to deliver in the first part of this meeting. Sean made a quick decision and decided to take a chance. This time Sean stood to make his point and just by doing so caught everyone's attentions.

Sean began by saying, "Blake, I appreciate your openness and honesty, but if you all would oblige me I would like to tell you a story." This caught the group by surprise because Sean had never begun any meeting or lesson he wanted to teach in such a serious manner. With that Sean continued, "What I am about to share with you is quite personal and I would ask that this stays in the room."

He paused for effect, and after seeing that he had everyone's attention, he proceeded to tell his story. "Many of you are aware that my wife passed away several years ago, but what some of you may not know is that the primary cause of her death was alcoholism. Kate's struggles started years ago when I first became a CEO and we found ourselves married to the job. The number of work-related events on our calendar meant we were often out two or three times a week at social events where drinking was common. We both probably overdid it, but we were able to control it—for a time, anyway. Things began to spiral out of control about nineteen years ago when..." Sean's voice trailed off as he felt the burning shame of what he had done once again.

The room became very quiet, and most began to feel anxious at what they were about to hear.

"The reason why things changed is because...I had an affair with another woman," Sean finally admitted in front of the group.

This stunning revelation about their highly respected leader was met with shock across the room. It was Jim Piper who uttered, "Say it ain't so."

"Kate sensed something was wrong and when she finally confronted me, I told her the truth. I had betrayed her sacred trust. No matter how good the sex was it was not worth the pain and suffering I caused. The pressure and guilt associated with such a terrible mistake was unbearable for both of us. My way to deal with this problem was to bury myself in work; my wife buried herself in the bottle."

The team seemed conflicted as they were trying to digest this information about their beloved leader.

"As the drinking began to take a physical toll," Sean explained, "Kate agreed to seek help. She tried valiantly to conquer the alcohol, but it proved to be too strong. Still, my Kate didn't give up. Finally, after her third try at rehab, she had success and remained off of alcohol until the day she died."

"Then how did Kate die?" Sister Jeannie asked as gently as she could.

"As the clinicians in the room probably know," Sean explained as his voice cracked with sadness, "when my Kate got the flu, her body was so worn out from all the drinking, it just couldn't fight it off. She passed a month later."

In front of their very eyes, the team was witnessing their leader become very human with each new part of the story he revealed.

"My Kate was a remarkable woman and she finally shared with me the reason for her success with quitting alcohol. Do you know what it was?" Sean asked, looking directly at Blake. "She forgave me."

Blake was uncomfortable with Sean's stare since it was his comments that had precipitated this revelation from Sean but he did not look away.

"As long as she held on to her anger," Sean continued, "she needed the alcohol to help her cope. But then one day something clicked for her and she realized that I was a *human being who had made a mistake*. Suddenly she could see that I loved her as I always had; I had simply made a bad decision. It was a terrible decision, but my Kate was able to forgive me for it." Sean's voice trailed off again until he quietly added, while looking down at the floor, "Unfortunately, my children never did."

Tears were now running down Sean's face as well as those of several others in the room. He knew this was a very sensitive and personal subject to be sharing, but he felt he needed to do so in order to help everyone understand that anyone can make a mistake. Sean continued, "My Kate did not have to forgive me, but she did, and as a result I was able to get my life back on track. In fact, without Kate's forgiveness I venture to say I would have never lasted in my career for as long as I did. Without Kate's forgiveness, I most likely would not be here with you today. And that is how I learned the hard lesson of forgiveness and second chances."

Blake spoke first in an unsteady voice. "Sean, I never meant any disrespect to you. That was a brave thing you did just now, and I feel like a total heel for my comments earlier."

Sean replied, "Blake, I only shared my story in the hopes that it will help you and everyone here to understand why I am asking you all to consider being open to forgive and give others another chance."

Blake looked back at Sean through moist eyes, "I do. And I am sure someday I will need to be forgiven. I only hope the person that I need that forgiveness from can be as gracious and kind as your lovely wife Kate."

Sean smiled and said, "Thank you for the kind words. I think it's important to be able to forgive—Kate taught me that. But what I also learned from that horrible situation was the importance of recognizing when you are standing at an intersection in your own life. And then taking the time to make the right decisions and use a tried and true process we all learned several meetings ago about how to arrive at the right decision. If I had done that earlier in my life, I would never have had that affair."

Sean looked down at the table where his cell phone was resting on a yellow legal pad with the name of every Futures Academy member written on it, and said, "I suspect that if Mike had used the decision-making process we all worked through together previously, he would not have taken that bribe either."

Sister Jeannie piped up, "Yes, 'how would Mike explain this decision to his wife and family?' would have been a deal breaker."

* * *

Sean gave the group a twenty-minute break and asked them to be prompt when returning because he had some good news to share. Sean could only imagine what the topic of discussion would be during the break.

Sean reentered the conference room exactly twenty minutes after the break began, and could not help but notice how everyone had gotten back early in hopes of learning more about the "good news."

Before Sean could begin, Kylene Knight spoke to Sean. "I know you have been in regular contact with Maria. Please let her know that we all want to help but we are not sure how. Please let her know too that we are all praying for her husband."

Sean said how much he appreciated those sentiments and added that Maria would too as she had been feeling very alone as she contemplated losing her husband and best friend. "Dan is in bad shape, but let's keep praying for him and hope for the best. His life is in God's hands now."

Sean turned to the rest of the group and motioned for the remaining stragglers after the break to sit down. "Now, for Blake's question about whether the Futures Academy is going to be ended."

After finding the notes for the next part of the meeting agenda, Sean shared what Pat Scott had shared with him about next steps. "I am happy to report that the Board met again over the weekend and voted unanimously on each of the next five points. First, for the immediate reinstatement of the Futures Academy." This brought a loud round of applause from the group. "Next, the Board voted unanimously to reinstate me as the Holy Spirit Health System Executive in Residence in support of the Futures Academy as well as to expand my role to oversee the Succession Planning for the entire Health System." That announcement drew many high fives. Sean finally had to calm them down by saying, "There is more. Third, the Board unanimously approved a two-year extension of Pat Scott's contract to make sure she is able to complete the turnaround efforts already under way." This was greeted with great excitement as well, which seemed to be building with each announcement.

"The fourth major decision made by the Board was to unanimously support the appointment of Rachel Pepper, MD, as the President & CEO of St. Mary's Hospital." That news got a standing ovation for Rachel and she was humbled and very thankful to everyone in the room for helping her get ready for such a great promotion. Once the excitement started to wane, Sean added, "Last but not least, the Board unanimously approved the appointment of Jim Piper as the Chief Human Resource Officer for the Holy Spirit

Health System." That led to another standing ovation and hugs all around for both Rachel and Jim.

Donna Reuss said, "Is that why you two were late coming into the meeting—so as not to spill the beans?"

Rachel responded, "We were sitting on pins and needles ever since Sean met with us this morning."

Jim added, "We also wanted the group to know that having completed our Career Plan Triangles made the decision to accept these wonderful career opportunities so much easier."

Sean had to remind everyone that not all of these announcements were made public yet and that they had to swear on the bible that they would not share the news until the announcement came out from Pat Scott, hopefully tomorrow. Everyone agreed to keep that promise, and Sean believed they would not violate his trust. Sean also knew he was holding back on one additional announcement that would be made in the near future.

Given where this meeting began, Sean was extremely happy to see this group celebrate its success and to enjoy being viewed by Pat Scott and the Board as the "future of the Health System." It was a sense of fulfillment like he had not experienced since he retired almost a year ago. His goal was to end the meeting on a high note, and it was safe to say he had succeeded with that goal.

Just as Sean was gathering up his notes and papers, his former assistant, Erin Carey, walked in with a poker face and handed Sean a note from Dr. Goldberg. Ever since getting the text from Sister Jeannie at the beginning of the meeting, Sean had turned his phone off so he could focus on the meeting at hand. The message read: "Dan Jacob's condition has taken a turn for the worse. Please come as soon as you can."

26

How to Handle a Crisis

As Sean raced out of the Executive suite at Divine Mercy Hospital, he was glad this meeting that had just concluded was at the hospital where Dan was a patient. This would enable him to get to the Neuro ICU within minutes. Just as he arrived on the unit, he saw Sister Jeannie standing at the nurse's station. He wondered how she beat him to the unit since he thought he had left the meeting in advance of anyone else. Maybe Sister Jeannie has talents we are all still discovering, he thought. As he approached, Sister Jeannie said, "Our special guest should be here within the next ten minutes."

Sean and Sister Jeannie made a plan that she would text him when everything was ready. Sean would be in with Maria and probably Dan's parents, and he did not want to disrupt any possible crucial conversations that might be going on by taking a phone call. Sean was wondering how things were going between Dan's parents and Maria since he was last with them. Sean knew from the previous encounter that Dan's parents were none too pleased with Maria, which could make the potential end-of-life decision that much more difficult to make.

Sean went into Dan's room and found Maria sitting on the side of his hospital bed holding her husband's hand. The look on Maria's face told it all. Maria looked up and said, "He's not going to make it, Sean."

A quick glance at the monitors and machines in Dan's room highlighted more medicines were being tried to save him but it appeared to no avail.

"Now I need to make a decision about whether to turn the machines off. I know they are keeping him alive and without them he will go, but," Maria faltered, "I'm not ready to lose him."

Sean could tell by the dark circles under Maria's eyes that she had not slept in a while.

"But I also know that if we wait too much longer, we won't be able to donate his organs. If we move quickly, he can help as many as eight different people."

Sean then asked, "How are Dan's parents feeling about the idea of taking Dan off life support?"

Maria said, "We had a lot of time together over the weekend, and we had a chance to clear the air on many things that had bothered us. What I came to realize is that they really love their son and they just want what is best for him. He is their only son, and losing him will be a terrible loss. They admitted they felt I was not the right spouse for their son, and yet they shared how he felt truly loved by me as evidenced by how he would always sing my praises each time they spoke to him on the phone. We all became more supportive of the idea of donating Dan's organs when the gentleman from the Gift of Life organization shared with us the information about the eight patients that would directly benefit from receiving them as well as countless others that would benefit from his bone and tissue donations. In spite of our great sorrow in losing Dan, we all realize what a legacy he would be leaving in helping those human beings. The real hard part is realizing that to help those patients means Dan has to lose his life."

As Maria spoke these words, Sean felt like her head knew what to do but her heart was still holding out hope for a miracle. Sean added, "Maria, do you remember when the Futures Academy discussed the nine different steps to making effective decisions? Maria responded "Sure, that is one of high-lights of all our meetings for me because it gave me a framework to make better decisions."

Sean continued, "If you think back on those nine steps, you have done steps one through eight over the past several days. I believe you know what the right decision is, and now all you have to do is the last step and that is to take action on the decision you made. I know that is easier said than done, but please know you will be making the right decision."

"You are right, Sean," Maria replied in a shaky voice. "It's time to move forward. At least something good can come out of this terrible situation."

Sean was so thankful to hear that Maria had come to some peace with the decision as he knew it was an incredibly difficult one.

Maria added, "The plan is to take Dan to the operating room in about an hour, at which time they will begin the organ donation process. We know they will be able to use his heart, lungs, kidneys, pancreas, intestines, and liver. In fact, the patient who will be receiving Dan's heart is a 29-year-old athlete and a father of three young children." At this point, Maria just broke down sobbing and fell into Sean's arms for physical and moral support. Maria fought through the tears and said, "Dan wanted us to have three children of our own someday." Her tears flowed for the next ten minutes without a word being spoken.

Sean finally broke the silence by saying, "We are all here for you," to which Maria replied, "But I feel so alone—I'm going to lose the only person that truly understood me. How am I going to go on?"

It was at this point that Sean asked if he could share something he learned from losing his wife. Maria replied with a nod of her head and so Sean began, "When I lost Kate, it was the toughest part of my life I had ever experienced. What saved me is something I learned about handling a crisis of any kind and I call it the '3 P's.'"

Maria had a quizzical look on her face, so Sean continued. "While preparing for and after my wife's death, I learned how lonely it can be when you feel like you are going through hell. I began to regain some control of my life by the first P, which is *place*. I needed someplace to go where I could get away from all of the life and death worries and just be alone. It could not be just any place but instead needed to be some place that had special meaning for me. For me, that special place was the John Hancock Observatory, day or night. The sweeping view of the whole city from up there enabled me to think, pray, and just disconnect for a while. There were times I even felt like my prayers were more effective because I was so high up and felt closer to God. I found after each visit that things seemed a little bit better, and to this day I still have my special place where I go to decompress and recharge."

"The second 'P' is *prayer*," Sean continued as Maria looked on. "For me, it was not the traditional prayers we grew up reciting as children, hoping God would hear us. It was more like me just talking to God and then being quiet so I could listen to what God wanted me to hear. This was a big change for me, but the quieter I became, the more I began to feel God's support and presence in my life. I felt like I was able to make sense out of everything that was happening in my life."

"The last 'P' has to deal with *people*. Traditionally, when things began to go 'south,' especially for the Irish, we began to withdraw into our own world and shut everyone else out. After Kate's death, it was like I was on a deserted island, which made my troubles feel even worse because I was isolated. It was only after I began to break out of my self-imposed isolation by joining a running group and getting back to playing golf with some of my old friends that I begin to realize how helpful it was to be around people while dealing with life's greatest challenges. As I began to understand the benefit of the three '3 P's,' I began to get my life back in order."

Sean paused and looked at Maria to see if what he had just shared was making any sense. Maria seemed so focused on what Sean had just said, with a far-away but serious look on her face, that Sean felt as if when he looked at her that he was looking directly into her soul. He could tell Maria was still searching for the answers she needed, but he hoped his words might offer some solace and guidance.

"Everything makes perfect sense," she said, "but I am all alone here in Chicago so I am not sure how I will handle the people part of your 3 P's."

Upon hearing this, Sean looked at his phone to see if Sister Jeannie had sent him any updates. As luck would have it, there was a text message from Sister Jeannie waiting for him. It read: "Standing outside the room. We will come in when needed." Sean stood and said to Maria, "There are many people who want to help you, but you are going to have to let them in to help you. I will help you, the members of the Future Academy will help you, and I bet others at work will also help. But in addition to all those I just named, there is someone else here who wants to help you. Is it okay if I bring that person in now?"

Maria was not sure what to expect, but because she trusted Sean, she said, "Yes." Sean walked over to the door and stepped outside for less than a minute to usher a special person into Dan's room. Maria was gazing at her husband when she heard a familiar voice say, "Maria, I love you."

As Maria turned her attention to the familiar voice, she saw her father, Xavier, standing in the hospital room. She first had a look of shock and then disbelief that her father was standing right in front of her. Xavier waited for some reaction from Maria, and as she began to stand, he stepped toward her with open arms and said, "I am so sorry for all of your pain." His arms just seemed to engulf Maria and his large chest muffled her sorrowful cry.

Maria gained some control and said, "Daddy, I am so sorry I didn't invite you to our wedding."

Xavier said, "Don't worry about things that are in the past. You are my daughter for life and I will always be here for you." It was just then that Maria remembered her father saying the exact same thing years ago when she was being so rude to him and acting just like her mother.

Maria added, "Daddy, I am about to lose the love of my life and I do not know what to do."

Xavier waited for a minute or so and then he said with confidence, "We will get through this together." Now Sean and Sister Jeannie were beginning to shed tears too at this heart wrenching life experience that was unfolding right in this hospital room.

Maria finally broke the silence and said, "I want you to meet Dan's parents, Beth and Keith Jacobs. They are really nice people, and I think you will really like them."

Xavier took Maria's hand and said, "I'm happy to meet the parents of Dan, and I want to thank them for raising such a wonderful young man that took such great care of you over the years."

Maria then said to her father, "Will you also be here when we have to say goodbye to Dan before they take him to the Operating Room?"

Xavier did not hesitate when he said, "I will be wherever you want me to be."

As Sean and Sister Jeannie were about ready to leave the room, Maria turned around and spoke directly to them and asked, "Since you two are the closest thing I have to family in Chicago and because you both have been so good to me over the past year, would you please be with us when we say our last goodbye to Dan?" Both Sean and Sister Jeannie said it would be an honor to be present to say their last goodbyes along with Maria, Dan's parents, and Xavier. Sister Jeannie left the room first. Before Sean left, he said that he would go and find Dan's parents and bring them back into the room. As Sean left, he heard Maria say to her father, "Why does life have to be so hard?"

* * *

About half an hour had passed when everyone gathered in Dan's room to say their last goodbyes before the staff took Dan to the Operating Room: Maria, Dan's parents, Sean, Sister Jeannie, Xavier, and Dr. Duncan and Dr. Goldberg. Dr. Goldberg turned down the volume on the monitors in the room so as to make these last few moments with Dan more peaceful. Next, Sister Jeannie asked everyone to gather around Dan's bed as she said some touching prayers. Afterward, she asked if each person present wanted to say their last goodbye and, if interested, to place a sign of the cross or some other religious symbol on Dan to help him on his journey to Heaven.

Sister Jeannie went first and made the sign of the cross on Dan's forehead and said some private prayers. The others followed, and each said their last goodbyes while making a sign of the cross on Dan's forehead. Seeing Beth and Keith saying their last goodbyes was particularly difficult for Sean being a parent of two children. Sean was surprised how Dr. Duncan became tearful since as a Neurosurgeon, he was very stoic and dealt with life and death on a daily basis. This just went to show how even the most highly trained physicians could have trouble losing a patient. Dr. Goldberg approached and traced a Star of David on Dan's forehead, consistent with the Jewish tradition. She too had tears in her eyes, which made Sean realize that every physician is touched in some way when they lose a patient that they have trained most of their lives to save.

Maria was the last to go and made a sign of the cross on Dan's forehead and then sat on the bed for one last hug, saying, "This is not goodbye; it is 'I will see you later.' Please watch over your parents and me until we can join you someday in Heaven."

* * *

As Sean left the hospital feeling down about losing Dan and seeing Maria, Beth, and Keith say goodbye to their loved one, he was also buoyed by two positive thoughts. The first was that eight patients would now have a chance at a better life as a result of receiving one of Dan's organs. The second was knowing that when Maria returned to work in a few weeks, Pat Scott would offer her the Health System CFO job as the replacement for Tina Blake. The reason why Pat Scott had agreed to delay the departure of Tina Blake was to give Maria time to recover from her loss and get back to work ready to take on her new responsibilities. Sean also felt good knowing that in one year's time, three original members of the Futures Group would have been promoted into Executive roles within the Holy Spirit Health System. "Not bad for one year's worth of work."

27

THIS IS FUN

IT WAS A beautiful fall Sunday, and three months had passed since Dan Jacobs' death. Sean finally got up the courage to visit Kate's memorial site, which he had not done since her funeral over three years ago. No one knew when Kate was buried that her ashes were to be taken to Ireland consistent with her wishes. Even though Kate's ashes were in Ireland, he still felt like Kate was with him at this blessed place.

There were two reasons why Sean had not been back to visit Kate's grave. First, he had to deal with his own guilt in the role he played in causing her death. The second reason was because immediately after Kate's burial services, his two children Katherine and Timothy told him that because of the harm he had done to their mother they never wanted to see him again. Every time he thought of visiting Kate's grave, he remembered that moment and could not bear to relive it. The pain Sean felt today upon visiting Kate in the cemetery was in fact as if they had said those words to him yesterday.

After saying some traditional prayers and picking a few leaves from around Kate's headstone, Sean sat down on the little bench next to her gravesite.

Instead of continuing with saying more traditional prayers, he followed the advice of Father Conor Lenahan, who had said, "Just talk to your bride as you would if she was physically present."

Sean began by saying, "A lot has happened in the past year that I wanted you to know. One of our rising stars, Maria, lost her husband as a result of a tragic accident. Yet, his death helped saved the lives of eight people waiting on various transplant lists. In fact, the patient who received his liver was a 56-year-old female who was a recovering alcoholic. It made me think of you, and I only wish you would have been a candidate for a new liver."

Sean paused, took a deep breath, and continued. "This Maria, who was estranged from her father for many years, reunited with him as he came to town to help her deal with the loss of her husband. Since that time, her father has relocated to Chicago and is working as an IT trouble shooter at one of the local banks. He is incredibly proud of Maria, who has been promoted into the role as CFO for the Holy Spirit Health system and is doing great professionally as she works through her personal grief."

Just then a fall breeze blew some additional leaves by Sean's feet, which he picked up and placed in his jacket pocket.

"There is a strange irony here, though, Kate. Maria started out on the wrong path and managed to turn it all around. My biggest disappointment is Mike Polaski, who started out looking to be a rising superstar and then made a series of bad decisions that torpedoed his career. He is serving an eighteen-month prison term for taking a bribe, but I visit him a couple times a month and check in on his family regularly. I am even helping his oldest daughter learn the finer points of softball. Who knows? Maybe she will be able to play for our beloved Cubbies someday. My hope is that her father, Mike, will be able to get his life back together and return to being the dad and the person God meant him to be."

"As for my job, I am having the time of my life teaching the next generation of leaders. In fact, I am working on a special project that only Pat

Scott, Sister Elizabeth, you, and I know about. The project is to get our own Maryanne Richmond ready to become the next CEO of Holy Spirit Health System. Pat has agreed to stay on until Maryanne is ready, and it's my job to get her prepared for her next career opportunity. This is really fun, and I feel blessed to have this opportunity."

Just then, a worker from the cemetery passed close by as he was checking on the American flags that were strategically placed on the gravesites of all the military veterans. Sean marveled at what a beautiful tradition it was to continue to honor those who gave their lives in support of their country.

"You would also be proud that I shared with Maria our 3 'P's' approach when dealing with life's challenges. Maria has really embraced each one of them and so have I. In fact, being here makes me realize how I want this to become my place to visit to get away so I can disconnect and try to make sense out of life. Being here makes me also remember how you always said that there was nothing more important in life than family. Seeing how Maria and her father have reunited made me realize that I need to try and reconnect with Katherine and Timothy. I know I screwed up and I have made it worse by not trying to repair the damage I caused before now. But I commit that before my visit to you next week, I will reach out to both of our children."

Just then, a cloud passed in front of the warm, fall sun, which sent a chill through Sean. As he stood, he reached into his pocket and pulled out twenty-eight pennies and placed them on top of Kate's headstone. Sean ended this visit by saying, "I kept up your tradition of picking up lost pennies I found since you always felt they were a sign from God that something good was about to happen. With each penny I find, I also take them as a sign of how lucky I am to have you as part of my life. Since the day you died, I have found these twenty-eight pennies and I want to share them with you. I will continue to keep up your penny tradition until we meet again in Heaven. I love you, my beautiful Bride. I miss you."

Sean bent down and slowly placed each penny, one by one, on the cool slab of marble that served as Kate's memorial. He could hear each one making a crisp sound as he created three symmetrical rows of nine pennies. As he placed the twenty-eighth penny in a new fourth row, he chuckled at the reminder that life wasn't always tidy or perfectly neat. He knew too, seeing space for eight more pennies in that last row, that it was time to go out and collect some more.

NOTES

NOTES

NOTES

NOTES

NOTES

NOTES

NOTES

NOTES

NOTES

NOTES

CPSIA information can be obtained at www.ICGtesting.com
Printed in the USA
BVOW01s0617110414

350333BV00001B/1/P